The Color of the Heart

What use are metaphors if slavery is not a metaphor,
if death in the River of the Dead is not a metaphor,
if the Death Squadron is not?
                                    — *Ernesto Cardenal*

We are more than we know.
                                    — *H.D.*

SUSAN SHERMAN

The Color of the Heart:

Writing from Struggle & Change 1959-1990

CURBSTONE PRESS

This book is lovingly dedicated to

SONIA MARRERO

Dear friend and comrade
who never gave up the fight

This publication was supported in part by donations,
and by grants from The National Endowment for the
Arts and the Connecticut Commission on the Arts, a
state agency whose funds are recommended by the
Governor and appropriated by the State Legislature.

These works have appeared in: *Conditions, IKON,
Mulch, Heresies, Shango de Ima, With Anger/With
Love, Big Deal, Women Poems Love Poems, American
Poetry Review, El Corno Emplumado, Women Brave
in the Face of Danger, Off Our Backs, WIN, Learning
Our Way, An Ear to the Ground, Naming the Waves.*

ISBN: 0-915306-90-5
Library of Congress number: 90-81429

Distributed to the trade by
THE TALMAN CO.
150 Fifth Avenue
New York, NY 10011

CURBSTONE PRESS
321 Jackson Street • Willimantic, CT • 06226

CONTENTS

THE COUNTERFEIT REVOLUTION:
McLuhan, Derrida, Lacan

CREATIVITY & CHANGE

INTRODUCTION

Sometimes, rarely, one is asked to perform some task so real, so sweet, so important in its alignment of history, that the first question invariably is: were you speaking to me? Is it really me you want to do this thing that others would surely do better? That's what I felt when Susan asked me to write an introduction to the book you have in your hands. Yet there is reason enough for me to say these words. Susan is a writer of experience and thought, and a facilitator of ideas, events, ways of seeing, whose work warrants a much wider recognition than it's had. Amazing as it is, this will be the first collection in which a really solid span of her multiple gift is available to us.

By multiple gift I mean a sensibility and craft that move through several genre: the finely-made poem, always clear yet surprising in its inner complexity; the prose poem, perfectly balanced between verse and story; and the essay, powerful both in scope and in the breadth of its revelation. The very nature of this volume — mixing these three written forms, which are generally kept safely separate — speaks profoundly of Susan's willingness to risk. Indeed, I believe this is one of her most important statements, whether it be as a thinker, writer, editor, teacher, organizer: her willingness, no, her insistence, on going one step further. Taking the risk.

Beyond that, Susan is a friend, a friend with whom I have shared work, dreams, connections, history, a deep friendship over many many years. In 1963 publishing some of her early work in *El Corno Emplumado*/The Plumed Horn (a bilingual literary journal I co-edited out of Mexico City in the sixties); our trip together to the Cuban Cultural Congress in Havana in 1968; our meeting in Managua for the fourth anniversary of the Sandinista revolution in the summer of 1983; and now again — and frequently — since I returned to the United States in 1984.

The first thing I want to say about Susan Sherman is that she is a visionary. And I do not reduce the term to its New Age ethereality. She is a visionary rooted in the most substantial of

7

forms, ideas which seem natural — impossible to dispute — today, but which years ago when Susan first spoke them brought her isolation, pain, silences, friends and co-workers who turned away, others who could not be expected to understand.

Throughout the sixties there was the first IKON, one of very few among the great renaissance of "little" magazines that really looked seriously at the problem of creative expression as a social phenomenon and printed exciting, important, and beautiful work in a coherent and responsible fashion. Not accidentally. Not haphazardly. Out of purpose. A purpose so well conceived, understood, rational in its dream, that it was anathema to many. One can go back to that first run of IKON and find — rare in the magazines of the period — that almost every selection sings out of a newness and truth still new — and still true.

Areas of Silence (Hespiridian Press/Hardware Poets Theater, New York City, 1963) remains as a gathering of Susan's own work from those years. A slim book. All but forgotten.

And the seventies brought a coming together (as they did for so many of us). A reaching out of the isolation. An attempt at reconciling some of the alienations. An initial breakdown of the barriers. Now there were others — mostly women — touching the spaces Susan had uncovered, so alone, through the preceding years.

Rooted in her knowledge of contemporary philosophy and poetry, but moving their ideas through her own particular sensibility and experience, what Susan had been saying for years about language began to make sense in a way more writers (and others) could understand. Her concern for the unity of content and form was suddenly more broadly shared. And Susan's feminism and lesbian identity not only found community, but moved from the pain of outsiderness to link up with a movement which is, today, at the forefront of this nation's creativity and change.

Creativity and change. This duality has been a logo for Susan's work. When colleagues at the old IKON walked away from her because she went to Cuba and came back to tell of the truth she found there; when "sisters" too left her standing almost alone because she saw a system (and not men) as the enemy; and when sectors of the "righteous" left disregarded her presence because she was a woman who understood the power of women in history; Susan simply kept on working, making the connections, bringing the visions together. As with many others who have traveled similarly pioneering roads, the work was not without deep personal cost: an ulcer, loneliness, ceaseless work.

With Anger/With Love (Mulch Press, Amherst, Mass., 1974) and *Women Poems Love Poems* (Out & Out Books, Brooklyn, 1975) speak for Susan's poetry in the seventies. And *Shango De Ima* (Doubleday, New York City, 1970), an adaptation she made of a Cuban Yoruba theatrical production written by Pepe Carril, first performed La Mama in New York City.

In the eighties Susan launched a second series of IKON. The revival of the magazine as a women's forum, in its first ten issues consolidating a statement of remarkable intensity in the world of contemporary creativity. Womanlove sings alongside Central America and Africa in its pages. Third World women, inside and outside the continental confines of the United States, show us they are currently pushing the outer edge (as the best of the lesbian cultural movement did a few years back). And IKON is not limited to the written page. Susan, as editor and central creative force, has facilitated a series of programs in which these connections have come to life (including that memorable historic event "Making the Connections" based on a special section in IKON #3: "Women in Struggle:Seneca, Medgar Evers, Nicaragua.")

In IKON Susan pays attention to the multicultural nature of our thought and action. You won't find an issue that doesn't feature the work of African American women, Indian and Hispanic women, Asian-Americans, lesbians and heterosexual women, mature and beginning writers, surprise contributions from places like Nicaragua's Atlantic Coast or the Marshall Islands. In an important issue, "Art Against Apartheid: Works for Freedom" (once more against the opposition of those for whom the formulaic is more important than the meaning), Susan

9

insisted on including the work of men who had participated in the original Art Against Apartheid readings upon which the collection was based.

Again, genre considerations are meaningless if they stand in the way of creativity and change: a powerful photo essay on Tompkins Square turned war zone reminds us that art and life do not imitate one another; they are often one and the same.

Very much in this tradition is Susan's latest book of poems, *We Stand Our Ground: Three Women, Their Vision, Their Poems*. It's the first IKON book and includes work by Kimiko Hahn and Gale Jackson as well as by Susan herself. A collection merging the voices of an African American lesbian, a heterosexual woman of Japanese-American and German origin, and a Jewish lesbian, makes for exciting reading. All three poets speak in uniquely personal ways.

But the most interesting feature of *We Stand Our Ground* is the long conversation with which the book opens. In it, these three women explore with one another — and for the reader — their memories of beginning to write, their politics and feminism, what poetry means in their lives. Again, the risk is there. And taking it pays off.

Susan is also a teacher, in the deepest sense of that word. Whether it's teaching philosophy in universities and colleges or poetry in the New York Public schools, or just sharing her knowledge of literature and art with friends who seek her help, she is always willing and available to offer practical as well as theoretical advice. Recently I was in an office in New York City's midtown and Susan's name came up in a conversation. An older woman, realizing we are friends, said: "She wouldn't remember me. Years ago I was one of many students. But she made a difference in my life, and I'll never forget her!"

The poetry and prose in *The Color of the Heart* speak fully for themselves. But I don't want to shy away from the responsibility of saying something about these poems and essays.

Few collections use introductory epigraphs more applicable to the voice projected in the book: Ernesto Cardenal's

> . . . what use are metaphors if slavery is
> not a metaphor, if death in the River of the
> Dead is not a metaphor, if the Death Squad
> is not?"

Commitment to life, in language. And H.D.'s

> We are more than we know.

The ultimate in our recognition of ourselves as women, weighted by a history of not knowing. Affirmation of the discovery which will finally place us on the road to being.

Moving through this volume, you will make a journey. The journey of a woman's life, and of a particular time. The life is only half over, but it's been lived thus far to its limits. And lived not only in the strong music, the risks and discovery; lived also in the fear, the doubts, the questions which she has not been afraid to ask — even when the answers do not readily surface.

In "Beginnings" (powerfully situated at the end of the book) Susan tells us:

> If you ask for nothing, that is exactly what
> you get. Even if, on the other hand, you lay
> out your demands, your heart, inch by inch,
> anxious for negotiation, ready for compromise,
> the result is often the same. But at least
> something is spared.

Also to take the challenge. We need each other.

> . . . If she were an umbrella, what kind of
> weather would she conceal? If she were a
> road, where would she wind? If she were a
> color, would she be bright or dull? How
> many miles would you have to walk her be-
> fore you would begin to understand? How
> many times would you have to play her
> before you would begin to hear?

And from the same poem:

> I remember one day in spring when I
> realized for the first time that grass
> is green. For me it was a new way of
> being in the world . . .

Not of seeing, but of being.

> The easiest thing in the world — to forget,
> to lose the center. To fail to hold it
> together.

The intimate becomes general (the personal, political):

> . . . real futility, not what we each
> face, which is not futile because it is
> real, is part of us as human beings, and
> as part of our own life has meaning, but
> that other futility, that noise, which
> means nothing, because it is not needed
> here, is not a need here, is happening
> here, where it is not needed, when so
> close to us that need exists.

Digging to build a subway route not to meet human needs but the system's, only a few blocks from where a subway route is really needed. And the conclusion, from the same poem:

> . . . now I can begin to move, to speak. The way
> a person really moves. Not step by step through
> a series of events, incidents, people — but layer
> by layer, building, forming, assimilating a life.
> (My emphasis).

This collection's opening piece, "Home," will be central, I think, when Susan's work is measured, her offering fully appreciated. It is clearly the beginning of a book, an autobiography which I hope she will write one day, soon. What we have here doesn't just take the reader back through a woman's life, but through a generation, a particular group of creative people, a meaning. This is personal and political/cultural history in the deepest sense.

Then there is "Barcelona Journal," a jewel, one of the perfectly-tuned and turned high points in this collection. The movement through twelve prose pieces and poems, the journey — including the photographic images which are so much a part of the text — is not a voyage to another place. It is a voyage inward, a discovery of self, using the displacement produced by inhabiting a different space and culture. It is a reaffirmation of a life when the (camera's) eye is free to roam and focus, center, signal, reveal.

Susan puts language to use, uses language in a way both faithful to her tradition (Stein, Williams, Black Mountain, Berkeley speech, New York sound??) and stripped by her particular consciousness. One instinctively knows she is a careful poet, a poet of craft and breath, a poet who spends months (years?) on a piece, so that it will roll off the page or tongue as if the reader/listener has a part in the invention. I should say that hearing Susan read her work is a powerful experience. In both the making and the reading, she gives the event itself, not a description of the event:

> The ceiling swayed back and forth. The floor
> tilted, folded, rocking gently like a ship. I
> grabbed for a chair, anything to hold me
> steady. I clutched the door frame. "Why didn't
> you tell me it was so strong?" Colors shot from
> the walls. Straight and sharp. So thick you
> could hold on to them. I was drifting in time.
> I stepped through the second hand of the old
> clock on the kitchen wall and everything
> stopped. The only sound was a faint, monotonous
> hum. Gold showered from the walls. It's just
> like Baudelaire, I thought, and laughed. The
> radio sounded like Donald Duck. Stop, I directed
> with my finger. And it stopped. Everything that
> was "real." I rose into the silence, my head
> inches from the ceiling. Alison swore she saw
> me disappear.
>
> (from "The Death of a Friend")

The quiet passion of her words. And the unquiet passion:

> The hill is on fire. Orange rims it like the
> sun. It is such a clear day you can see the
> city in all directions. Houses poured into
> hills, until the hills themselves are really
> no more than waves of houses, frozen in cement,
> tile & brick — the color of muted earth...
> (from "Barcelona Journal")

Each of the six sections into which this book is divided recreate an experience of life, art, change. "The Color of the Heart" is deeply autobiographical, introducing the reader to this woman/poet, her life, her world. "Cuba, Chile, Nicaragua" moves out onto that larger terrain so many in this country ignore or see only in the most eurocentric way — as our media filters disinformation about who lives out there, what they think, how they see themselves and us. As long as we continue to know them as "other," we cannot know ourselves. This section contains the essay "Feminism & The Nicaraguan Revolution," one of the many places in which Susan successfully bridges the distance between ideas which we are taught are mutually exclusive, or antagonistic to one another.

In "Divisions," we are brought back to events and controversies of the seventies, asked to reexamine issues which remain intensely relevant today. Some readers will remember specific incidents; for them a refocusing from this perspective will be enlightening. Younger readers will read this section as history, the history left out of our text books, erased from common memory. For them this constitutes the rare opportunity to look at process, rather than try to assimilate the facts that are so often passed off as "the way things were."

In the first section, fiction or the long prose poem predominated; in the second one of Susan's strong essays centers a number of short poems; by the third we are deep into Susan as essayist. The essay "Women, Identity, Sexuality: A Reexamination" (which I have taught many times) is the centerpiece for the fourth section: "Sexuality & Identity." The poems surrounding it are powerful reverberations of the echoing theme: how we are in the world. "Horizon" is a poem of Susan's I believe will be anthologized for many years to come.

The fifth section, "The Counterfeit Revolution: McLuhan, Lacan, Derrida," is pure essay: deconstruction and analysis. Susan takes on these three men, whose work informs sectors of both the left and the feminist movement, and walks us through what they are really about. This is "the emperor's new clothes" debunked, a stand requiring courage as well as a complex mind.

The sixth and last section, "Creativity & Change," is a real summing up. Here Susan is once again the poet/the essayist/the poet. "Freeing the Balance" is another extraordinary essay. "Beginnings" returns us to our own cyclical process. Time, space: they are not linear but spiral into the center and out to infinity.

I want to ask people to read each of the sections in this book as a complete experience; each has been structured so that its parts compliment one another in important ways. While the separate pieces stand alone, in each case the whole is more than the sum of its parts.

Finally, I do not want to talk away these poems, these ideas, these experiences. This experience, for again it is of a piece. I could not, and will not. Perhaps I have rambled too much already, in my desire to say: Susan Sherman sings to us here, for the first time in such a multifaceted range, with all the fullness of her wisdom and her spirit.

Margaret Randall
Albuquerque / 1987-1989

The Color of the Heart

HOME

No color. No sound. No movement. No thought.

The moment I realized what had happened, it was gone: like waking from a dream, but I was already awake, and the transition was instantaneous — if you can use the language of time in relation to something that is out of time.

It was in the spring of 1965. I was absorbed in writing. Several things were coalescing in my mind. I had just finished reading *Answer to Job,* Jung's analysis of the psychological development of God in which he sees, as does Rilke, the world as a representation of God in the process of "becoming." I was intent on the paradox evoked by this idea: "How is it possible for something to be complete, and in the process of completion at the same time?" when one afternoon, while reading in Paracelcus what I thought was totally unrelated material, I was literally thrown into the answer to my question. For an instant, I actually *experienced* time moving differently.

I was certain of only one thing: it was no illusion, no hallucination — my experience was real.

When I thought about it later the only thing I could say by way of explanation was that there exists a parallel sense of time in which we are heading toward a past yet to happen, while the future is behind us, already set — this parallel time running simultaneously with time as we ordinarily perceive it. Therefore all time *is* literally contained in every present moment; but even more, the present, being made up of future and past moments, has no meaning without both. I began to understand the use of paradox in religion, in Zen koans, and even in philosophical and Marxist dialectics: to draw students into a place where their questions can be answered only through direct experience.

I also understood something from that experience I hold to even more firmly now. Experience which comes from such an occurrence is *raw* experience, without moral, philosophical or religious content. I am convinced such experiences are neutral and, in isolation, only prove themselves. I really don't *know* what my experience meant, I could only speculate on it after the fact from who I am, where I was at.

When I tried to recount what had happened to me later that same evening to a friend, I started to shake and cry uncontrollably. For years that experience was a constant source of frustration to me. I tried to replicate it and couldn't. I was afraid to talk about it to anyone, afraid they would misinterpret what had happened — if they believed it at all. After awhile it began to fade. Two years later, in 1967, I would travel to Cuba and the experiences I would have there, however different, would in many ways parallel this one. Turn me around and be battered, too, if from other directions. As love had done to me also, when it finally came, when I was up to its demands.

I start with this particular experience because it changed my way of perceiving the world, because it is something I want to reach back toward, to fix in memory, to find again. As I would so many other experiences that shaped and will shape my life. That fade so easily in our society — a society which invalidates our idealism and memory, that affirms only the present moment, disembodied, without context, without history, denying us in the process our future along with our past.

One : Return

There is no such thing as an unnoticed event, a trivial subject. Only mountains are large, the sea. Things that have no consciousness, conscience, are not human. Our lives are made up mostly of an accumulation of small incidents: the crowded supermarket on a Saturday afternoon, a baby crying at three o'clock in the morning in an upstairs apartment, people marching miles on dirty New York streets protesting an unjust war, the touch of a lover's hand. Seemingly different, each one alone, a detail, but taken together an event with major importance, turning history in new directions.

During the summer of 1976, one month before I would turn thirty-seven, I made my way to Los Angeles, to the place I had once called home. After fifteen years of absence, I felt strong enough finally to face what had borne me, the place that had shamed and nurtured and frightened me both into silence and into words.

Los Angeles. "City of the Angels." In the forties, fifties, with its trappings of glamour, its obsession with plastic and what is large, it had seemed to represent the future — America's as well as mine. But now even that was gone. It was calm, flat, with the dullness of a person grown old in emptiness, with money but without resources, imagination, wonder.

Memories flood my mind. Doors. Opening in/out. In one place, gray, shabby. In another, enameled, polished, without blemish, human presence, the trace of a human hand. Feeling, no, knowing somehow if they knew my thoughts, sensed me, what I really was, what I was about to become, they would take me from my life, lock me up as I had locked them out.

And then emerging, slowly, almost without consciousness, into other places, another life: Berkeley, London, New York, Cuba, Chile, Barcelona, Nicaragua. Rooted in another way — not in places now, but people, a person, my person. As people change differently than buildings, cities, avenues. Something remaining, always with us, providing continuity, understanding, depth.

Not the stuff of philosophy, of "higher thought," logic, the mind? To the contrary, the very stuff of philosophy, poetry, change. The white hair of my mother finally allowed at seventy to gray. The bent figure of my step-father thinned in his sickness of body and mind. Built, not on words alone, but on the violence of action and years.

On the face of it, returning home was a simple task, a matter of steps. Walking across a threshold, into a room. But it had taken me more than a decade to prepare for it. A young woman going through the Mexico City airport, destination Havana, 1968. Sweat pouring down my neck. Fear — and heat. 1961. Nights of terror on New York streets. Buildings dimming in and out of focus. Waking in the middle of the night. Dizzy. Sick. Anything for the sound of just one human voice to pull myself back by. Just one human voice saying, "Susan." Calling my name.

But even those events were simple compared to this one uncomplicated task — to put one foot in front of the other and slowly cross a plain wooden threshold and look two old people, my parents, in the face.

Not the stuff of philosophy? Yes, the very stuff of philosophy. The cut green grass, razor sharp, seemingly endless, yet only ten square feet. The apartment, clean, ordered, showing signs of decay. Not in age — everything new, spotless, the multitude of painted flowers over the white brick fireplace, the seven potted plants each in their own particular space: the arrangement of ashtray (silver), cigarette lighter (silver), picture frame (silver), on a black enameled table. Not in age, in meaning. Everything rising to and resting finally, rootless, on the surface. A house resting on the surface of things, tied to nothing, growing old. As we all grow old, begin to resemble more and more ourselves, become more and more ourselves — whoever we might be.

My parents were immigrants, children of immigrants. My mother the youngest in her family, the only one born in the United States. My stepfather born in Russia in 1905, coming here at the age of eight. Jews, fleeing from Russia, Poland, the pogroms, the army. My uncle buried for three days under a pile of corpses, crazed with pain and fear, afraid to breathe, to show life. My father, my mother, my uncle. The old transplanted. Their enemies now reborn in them, until they became caricatures, finally, of much of what they had tried so desperately to escape.

There is nothing on this earth with one meaning only, one way of approach, one point of view. We do not exist as "one," even to ourselves. We are, each one of us, a community, collective, a set of relationships, a world. A world that must reach out to other worlds or else, in its turn, oppress and decay.

Contradiction is defined in *Webster's Dictionary* as a "statement in opposition to another; denial." "...a condition in which things tend to be contrary to each other; inconsistency; discrepancy," "a statement that contradicts itself." In Aristotelian logic, self-contradiction is not allowable, a statement cannot be both itself and its opposite at the same time — both A and not A.

In life, however, this is not the case.

If my parents had not come to this country, they would both long ago have been killed, and I would never have been born. It was their effort that bought me my education, cleared for me my space. These are not easy sentences to write, knowing this, knowing their struggle. Things are not one, not simple, in motion. Driven, in fact, into motion by the very contradictions we hold within us, as people, as a society, as a nation. Subject always to the laws of change.

What drives us forward. What holds us in place.

But motion does not mean just a change in place. Contradiction is also the opposition of things at the *same* time, in the *same* space. Holding multiplicity in suspension. As I tried once to hold my mother, as she could no longer hold me.

As I finally turned away.

What moves a person, a people, a nation: In 1939, six weeks after I was born, Germany attacks Poland. On September 3rd, Britain and France declare war. I don't remember what happened those first years, I was too young. The real effects would come later for me — circled in warnings, cloaked in advice.

Watch your accent, how you speak. Watch your inflection, the emotion in your words, your hands. Your walk. Watch the way you walk. At their center, they will always hate you. In moments of intimacy, it will always be there. You are Jewish, a woman. Be invisible. What you do can turn back on your family, a whole people. Don't stand out. Don't draw attention to yourself. Hide. Hide. Hide...

Violence. And fear. It is 1945. My family is gathered around an old radio that takes up at least an eighth of the room. There is tremendous excitement. I am six years old. We hear a minute by minute report of the dropping of the first atomic bomb. Afterward I am sent to describe the event to my older sister who has the measles, with the double-purpose of also exposing myself to the disease. That was the way of it then — "getting rid of it while young." Both events take on equal importance.

They are treated the same.

For most of my early years I felt caught between two worlds: two mothers, two fathers, two religions. But perhaps that is a primary motivation to express oneself through art. The feeling, not of alienation, but of not fitting securely in any one position. Because our expectations become somehow different. The hardest things to get past — expectation, need. As we always pick up the threads of what supports our own theories, beliefs, options.

It was after my trip to Cuba in 1967, I think I began for the first time to recognize a real alternative, the tangible existence of other people, the possibility of lasting change. Not that I had not already begun to gather myself in, to find a different space, first in Berkeley and then in New York, but understanding that new place as preparation really for this discovery — what it meant to struggle together with other people, *with people different from myself*, to change, not only myself, the circumstances and people connected with my own life, but the world around me. To change it with and for other people. It is the necessity of that lesson that sinks in ever more deeply, that rises in flashes, brilliant and then gone. Changing but consistent. Providing continuity, understanding, depth.

So my search was not there, in my parents' house, no longer my home, in that room empty of everything except memories, but in my own being, the cells of my own body, my own mind. The threshold which takes real courage to cross — from oneself to the other. Not in retreat, barricaded, but going forward, recapturing meaning, wresting it from the violence that conceals it.

The outward appearance. The inner reality. Inside the body of a small child, inside the body of a nation, a seed had been planted and was waiting to be born.

Unlike Los Angeles, Berkeley was a place I approached with love, not fear. I looked forward, after seventeen years, to once again walking streets that had changed so much in my life, of revisiting places in which I had moved, had grown. I saw myself sitting in favorite cafes, movie theaters, one particular spot on the wide university lawns, a remembering surrounded by detail — sights, smells, sounds. A tangible reconstruction of the past.

And I remembered nothing. Recognized nothing. Was familiar with nothing. Was thrown into a strange, an alien place.

The magic in my memory alone. The rest gone cold for me. The years gone cold.

If by some miracle I were to suddenly, mysteriously, confront myself seventeen years ago, walking down those streets, is it possible I would not have recognized, been familiar to myself? That I would be an absolute stranger to myself as I was then; in the same way that self might not recognize me as I am today.

And, if so, how can I write about what took place so many years ago? How can I paint an image of what *I* was, much less describe the people, the events that helped shape what I am today?

But fortunately people, events are not places — less solid, they are also more sure. That is why the necessity to write it out becomes even greater, in spite of the limitations of memory, the propensity of memory to bring everything up to date.

So I will start with Berkeley, the time that was most important to me. I will try to find that double, that "other," which was also me, try to set her down, set it straight. Before it dissolves completely, vanishes completely, past even the reconstruction of my imagination. Before even the memory, the fullness that remembers is gone.

Two : Arrival

To discover that the world you have known all your life, you have known since childhood, is not the only world. To discover that the people who surrounded you, their values, their ethics, are not the only values and ethics, is probably the most important discovery in a person's life, because it is to discover the possibility of not one, but many alternatives, it is to discover the possibility of choice.

Berkeley, 1959. As if everything had been a prelude to that, as if that was the point from which, in the future, I would go both forward and backward in time. As I became aware of sound, smell, touch, my own form and the form of the world around me. As my life began to take on meaning, a consciousness, a physicality missing before. As I began to slowly separate things out. Identify them. Give them names. As I began to identify myself. Name myself. Separate myself out finally from the world around me. Assume a posture mine alone. It was the first time I knew there was a way of life I wanted to be part of. The way you know the first time you are in love and no matter what you might have once thought to the contrary, you have never been in love before.

And so, in a very real way, I was born in Berkeley, California, 2478 Telegraph Avenue, in 1959, in a rented room (shared bathroom, shared kitchen, shared living room — at night another bedroom). A magic place to my uninitiated eyes, and even now, decades later, the traces of that magic remain. As if every fantasy I had ever had, transformed into a shape I had never considered, was coming to life. (Fantasies being based on our present reality, never on what we cannot know.) And the other world, the world of childhood, of Los Angeles in the 40s and 50s, simultaneously receding into the background and coming into focus, was beginning also to assume a shape I could recognize and finally start to understand.

Each important place in a person's life always seems to relate to one special sense, has something unique you can identify and remember it by. In Berkeley it was smell: the smell of Eucalyptus after dark — a night scent carried by a night breeze. If you could, for a moment, imagine the aroma of a real Mexican *flauta,* (chicken or cheese wrapped with tortilla, delicately fried, smeared with guacamole and sour cream, take out 40¢) eaten with a pint of beer for dinner while sitting in an old, but large, kitchen with a stove built in 1919 — a brass plate attesting to its age on the oven door. If you could crunch your meal between your teeth — hiding it from Thornbranch, a cat so-named because as a kitten he was rescued from a paper bag a junkie had tied him in, swinging him round and round his head, so that for months whenever someone moved too close to him he jumped on them and clung like a thornbranch — kitten claws clutched into clothes, legs, whatever was exposed and close. If you could touch the hot burning streets in October — summer being mostly cool — or survive the months in winter when there was continual rain, the sky looking like an inverted gray bowl on the horizon. If you could do these things, then you might be able to sense the Berkeley of the late 50s and early 60s — even before the free speech movement — echoing to the brand new political organizing call of SLATE.

This was the Berkeley of poets, political activists, jazz musicians, students, and just hangers on. The Berkeley of revelation and division, of cheap wine and hamburgers and stolen food, of old movies (two shows a night and three on Sundays), of the House Un-American Activities Committee demonstrations, of bigotry and idealism, of violence always just beneath the surface, of first sex and first love — two very different events. Of a history even then.

Across the bay in San Francisco, North Beach was crowded with people listening to the revival of an ancient tradition in poetry, spoken poetry, which had been left in the trail of the Beats and the "San Francisco Renaissance." Because what Allen Ginsberg and Gregory Corso, what Lawrence Ferlinghetti and Robert Duncan had left behind them, what they had created around them was a world. A world you pressed against like a child presses against a candy store window, the way I had pressed my nose against the window of an old Cafe in Berkeley the year before and had wanted and been afraid to and then finally, tentatively, entered, to find I had entered a place of birth like the glass mirrors in a fun house, always leading forward, a series of windows really, a new kind of space.

Because poetry, because art, is a way of life opening into other ways of life, with its own rules, its own set of directions, its own set of traps.

A friend of mine told me at the time, when I was worried about my own poetry, trying to find a new style, a new way of speech, I could never change my poetry unless I changed myself. Skill must be learned, a knowledge of language, of words, of form must be reached, but form not only shapes the content the life of the artist gives it, it also grows out of the content — the life — of the artist. Because the whole search in the 50s and early 60s was a search for new forms, for new ways of seeing and feeling.

Even though she came to Berkeley in 1957, it was not until two years later things really began to change for her. She remembered her first impression of Berkeley the day she arrived. Everything seemed so small, as if she had been thrown back to her recognition at the age of ten of physically changing size. Coming home after a summer away and finding things mysteriously smaller: familiar things like a favorite book, a placemat, a milk bottle. But now it was different, it was houses and streets, cars and people that seemed to have shrunk in size. A second recognition, this time at 18 — of growing at the expense of things outside.

"Stop for a minute will you, I want to get out of the car."

Suddenly she seemed suffocated, as if the buildings on each side of her were walls which would momentarily start closing in. She felt panicked. She didn't want to go home, had nowhere else to go, but if she didn't get out of the car — immediately — she felt she would burst.

"What's the matter with you? We're going to be late."

The voice coming from the front seat of the car seemed disembodied, urgent. It only magnified her sensation of dislocation, of needing to be outside, to stand outside, quietly, for a moment, to establish her space.

"Please, just for a minute."

The car slammed to a stop. The driver obviously afraid she was going to be sick.

She got out, looked around. There is nothing worse than a strange city, where you know no one, have no roadmarks to hang on to, no favorite street where you know each turn, which leads with total predictability in any direction you choose to go.

Berkeley. What had driven her here anyway? She couldn't get into Stanford. Everyone knew they had a quota on Jews and besides her parents would have never put up the tuition. Not for one of "the girls." Even though, as it turned out, she would be the only one of her family to finish college. So here she stood in this strange place — not too far, but just far enough away from home. Little knowing just how far away it would finally become. She wrinkled her nose absentmindedly, a bad habit she had when disturbed, and stood there, frozen.

"What is the matter with you anyway?" Concerned, but annoyed. "We'll be at the hotel in a few minutes. If you're not going to be sick, please get back into the car."

By 1959, the city had assumed normal proportions. She had fitted herself comfortably into her new surroundings — her now magical place — this old gray room with the gray wooden door and the big bay window where she set her bed, jamming it carefully against three large window panes overlooking the street, the very place which a decade later would become an anti-war center, first destroyed by a bomb and then later, and with much more finality, by a wrecking truck. To be turned into a parking lot, where, on Sundays, peddlers gather to sell beads and moccasins, pottery and tofu pies.

The building had a reputation. It was a place where artists lived. The de facto building managers, two painters from New York, lived down the hall. She could not understand until years later when she moved to New York herself why they had three locks on their door, which were carefully checked every time they left the house. Not only didn't she have locks on her own door, most of the time it was just left open.

2478 Telegraph Avenue — four "apartments" on the second floor, four on the third. The first floor was occupied by a grocery store. Her own room was in a two room complex bordering a larger kitchen which she, Diane Wakoski and LaMonte Young shared with the occupants — two of them — of a small room in the front of the building. Max and his wife — whose name she never did know. They were very private, almost never left their room and were more like rumors than real people.

I try to recall her. This Susan of almost thirty years ago. Try to conjure up her face in my mind. I find myself as frozen as she was so long ago, looking around her at new streets, new people, smelling new smells, feeling a whole new kind of air striking at the surfaces of her skin. I look into my mirror, turning my own face from side to side, but it doesn't help, is a distraction really. Of course, she would resemble me, *being* me — at however young an age. But resemblance means nothing. A lesson I learned the hard way, returning to Berkeley after all those years to find it alien, even though outwardly it still looked pretty much the same.

I pick up a photograph of myself from that time. How conventionally we dressed, even as rebels, in relationship to the way we, all of us, dress today. I am wearing a skirt in the photo, have short brown hair, am sitting on a wide wooden table. My face looks so young to me, younger even than the twenty years it reflects. I reach toward it, touch it, as if to reach toward myself, as if to physically hold myself, those evenings — why is it always the evenings I remember best?

Poetry readings at night in a darkened apartment, a candle passed from poet to poet as we took our turns to read. Waiting in line for the one communal bathroom down the hall — that never seemed to bother me then, there was always another upstairs. A row of empty wine bottles, blue and white ceramic, converted into candlesticks, lining the borders of the walls. The dozens of men I slept with as part of the "sexual revolution." Those nights rising from a strange man's bed, seeing a pair of strange shoes, underclothes, on the floor beside my own. Or sometimes at dawn, dressing and leaving quietly before they could wake up — most often I had never even been asleep. Walking the empty streets to my own bed. My own place. Feeling a loneliness I had never experienced before, have never experienced since.

I often think years are not cumulative, somehow they are passed one after the other, like steps: in order to advance to the next, it being necessary to leave the last behind. This is why it is crucial now, at forty-nine, for me to reach across the years, to somehow communicate with that young woman, that self, who was once me. To make that connection. Not that I would want to send her advice, or even warn her — if that would somehow miraculously be possible. What good would it do and what alternative could I even now recommend? But to provide a security she could sense, a private place in herself she could turn to. Or perhaps it is really I who am looking for something from her. Something I have forgotten only she can tell me, only she can make me understand.

Those years in Berkeley she often had the sense of having been dropped into another universe. The way you feel almost always traveling to a foreign place — never believing you are going, never believing you are there, and when you return never believing you had gone. Constantly and secretly staring at small treasures you picked up along the way just to convince yourself, yes, you really were there. The feeling of being slightly out of contact, slightly out of touch. Although she had sometimes felt that in Los Angeles, at least in the early years, it didn't seem an unusual way to feel about Berkeley, which was after all a trip to unfamiliar territory. A world where people talked about dragons and witches, read Tarot cards, and lived the unknown and the unseen. It felt okay for her to be an observer there, as natural as it had felt unnatural at home, a place where you were, after all, supposed to belong.

She had often felt — at least from the time she consciously could remember feeling anything, certainly from the age of five, when she left on that long journey across a continent to the West Coast — she was an observer, secondary to the action taking place around her. It was the beginning of a realization which would come to her finally in New York: that being an artist often meant being literally two people — one constantly scrutinizing and commenting on the other. An almost schizophrenic state. The silent monologue. The constant observation of living detail, including yourself.

At its worst this feeling of disassociation would manifest itself in the inability to communicate, to connect. In sitting to one side. As she had trained herself to do as a child, hoping finally no one would notice her — she could stay outside the chaos, violence, which was her home. A helpful habit until it leapt out of control: the aversion to being touched, the inability to speak.

She felt this often those first few months in the new home she shared with Diane and LaMonte, people who were virtual strangers to her then, but would become pivotal to everything that happened to her from there on in. The silence came not from fear now, but from newness, from just wanting to see and learn. Not that she felt completely comfortable — she felt conventional, ashamed of her innocence, "square."

It bothered her for anyone to know at twenty she had never slept with a man, the acceptable condition for a "nice girl" where she came from, but not here, where people laughed and made jokes about "virgins." Being a virgin became the symbol of everything representing the world she had come from, so desperately wanted to leave and could only leave by becoming a part of this new world she had so recently discovered. The way you can sometimes eradicate the pain of a lost lover only by finding a new one.

Though often only a temporary solution, one that works.

So at an ordinary party on an ordinary night no more than two weeks after she had moved into Telegraph Avenue, no more than three months after her twentieth birthday, she decided to act. It was a warm night; everything seemed stuck together. Even the people at the party seemed somehow glued to each other, unable to come apart. She found this reassuring, it made her feel secure. She chose a teaching assistant in economics, a tall man, probably over six foot four. She liked tall men, although later she would joke that picking out one this big as her first lover was probably a mistake. She had a couple of drinks. Vodka. First with Ginger Ale and then straight. She decided before the night was out she would no longer be embarrassed by her inexperience, no longer unknowingly be the butt of jokes and snide remarks.

She walked over to him quietly, initiated a conversation; they began to dance. Before a half hour was out, they were kissing passionately on the couch, and she made her final decision to take him home. All she had was a cot, she hadn't had a chance yet to buy a bed; it would have to do. As they were going up the stairs to her room, she informed him she had never slept with a man before.

He stopped, looked a little startled. She was surprised how unemotional she felt. How removed. She had been far more nervous about far less important things.

"If you would prefer not to come up? Is it alright?"

"Oh, no, not at all. You just startled me." He was obviously delighted. "Although you really should be more careful. You never know who you could run into at a party like that.

"You're lucky it was me."

They went into her room, undressed, and he proceeded to perform with all the skill of a fledgling academic, accompanying each step with a comprehensive lecture on how a condom was properly fitted, (at least a half inch of empty space had to be left at the top), why it was essential for it to be used correctly, finally climbing on top of her with little effort and little grace. She had never seen a man naked before, not at home, where intimate moments of any kind were unknown, and hardly had a chance to see one then. It all seemed to happen so fast. There was no fear, just a kind of bewilderment, and then a few moments of really intense pain.

"Am I hurting you? I'm sorry, just hold on. It will be over soon."

He got off her, switched her to her side, explained this was another "popular position," was sometimes more comfortable, and proceeded to go through the motions again. It hurt less this time, although she was beginning to feel quite sore, and when he left she was glad to see him go, grateful he "couldn't spend the night." She was tired and needed to be alone and think.

When she went to the bathroom, she realized she was bleeding. She would continue to spot blood on and off for the next two days. She felt older, not unlike the first day she had started her period. Like she had passed through a certain rite. A ritual of blood. She was disappointed, but hadn't expected much really. Had oddly had no romantic notions after all. This night was just something she felt she had to do. She also learned something that night about sex, about herself, something she was to learn again and again even under very different circumstances. Between her and him now, at least for her, there was some kind of tie. Enough even though she really had no desire ever to sleep with him again, she felt genuinely betrayed when she learned, bumping into him accidentally one day on the street, he was married, and "couldn't see her again."

Sex became something quite different for her now. Before she had gotten very aroused, had almost always come to orgasm, through close contact or being touched. Now sex suddenly became more personal and impersonal at the same time, less sexual and involved with many other things.

She also enjoyed finding herself attractive to men. Having three or four or more of them constantly around courting her. Up to that point she had really considered herself a wallflower, not the kind of woman who was popular with men. It wasn't looks, she just didn't have the kind of sexuality, the flirtatiousness that appealed to the boys in high school or in her first two years in college. She had had dates, had gone steady, have actually at one point almost considered marriage, but she was pronounced too serious, too smart and told it would never work, "good-bye." Now, it seemed she had found men who liked her spirit, her brains, and, she had to be honest about it, the fact she was available and would sleep with them. She hardly ever went out with them more than a couple of times. Some of the more sensitive ones obviously felt the same way she *had, felt some kind of lingering bond: a sentiment she now rarely returned, which she found made her even more desirable, more attractive to them. Most of them treated her well — there was a surprising amount of impotence — although some experiences were disagreeable and came very close to rape.*

She slept with all of them. Finding that easier finally than saying no.

She had a reoccurring dream during those years which would continue to haunt her. She dreamt she was paralyzed, rigid — awake but unable to move or speak. She was convinced when she closed her eyes she could see through her eyelids, could note every detail of the room around her. She woke up many nights in the middle of the night, sweating, forcing herself awake. Afraid to return to that state of unconsciousness, of helplessness. Sometimes a voice intruded, sometimes laughter. More often it was just her, alone, in the night. She wondered if that was what death was like. Why so many people feared being buried alive.

Fear. Fear builds over years. I don't remember then really being afraid except in sleep. At least not of new things. Things for which I had no reference. There was memory of early years of asthma and croup. Hours trapped over an inhalator with a towel circling my head, the fumes still lingering in my brain. And of one warm summer night swimming in a country pond with a half-dozen friends when one of them jumped on my back as I was coming up for air. The sensation of my lungs bursting, as I was pushed further and further below the surface. Every muscle and cell in my body straining, pushing, fighting. The final breaking through to the surface. The accompanying horror at what I had experienced. Barely able to take it in. Silenced, not relieved.

And fear of my father, of being assaulted by my father. Sleeping for one whole year in my early teens with a baseball bat by my side. Making sure I was never alone in the house. And later never going home for vacation if I could help it.

Until finally I never went home at all.

I see these echoes most in situations that frighten me now. Anything that has to do with losing my equilibrium. Fear of

34

elevators and subways. Of bicycles and roller skates. Fear of losing contact. Of getting high. Of that sensation of choking, of not being able to breathe. The first time a woman tried to make love to me, I pushed her away. Even though no more than six months later I would look at a woman myself and want to make love to her. Perhaps fear is an indication of how deep something can reach inside you. Of where you are truly vulnerable.

What touches you most. What makes you afraid.

But for the moment most of these events were in her past. Now something had just begun. She thought to herself that night in early September, sitting alone in her room, staring at a small spot of blood on an empty cot where minutes before two bodies had lain: "I am here," She thought. "Finally, I have arrived."

THE FOURTH WALL

1.

From which direction does the wind flow? It flows from the East. From which direction does the wind flow? It flows from the East and into my hands.

Analysis. Cross-reference analysis. The age of analysis. Psychological, philosophical, poetic analysis. Not the event, but the picturing of the event.

Days, dwarf-like, with tinsel hats. America. Orange, sticky, matted.

My father was from Russia. When he was a small child, he crossed the borders of his country with a half-dozen other refugees. He often spoke of the town in which he was born. A small town. Long rows of hot, sandy streets. Plain one-story buildings. The cries of Cossacks cutting through the level dirt walks of his home.

"Jew," they yelled, and he ran. "Jew," they yelled, and he ran across a continent. "Jew," they yelled, and he ran across an ocean.

They never really believed they had left for good. They never even learned to speak the language. But my father learned. When he was twelve, he learned — my mother waiting for him across the length of a continent.

How many years does it take? In this, my sweet-smelling land. In this, my sweet-smelling land, where there is no question of time.

They say a desert is an uncultivated region without inhabitants; a wilderness. A dry barren region largely treeless and sandy. This is only partly true. My desert is decorated with pinecones and exotic spice. In spring, the cactus blooms into small, pink flowers. My evenings are colder than it is possible to imagine. I take off my clothes at night so I may lie naked. Next to the warm body of my desert. My beautiful, beautiful desert.

2.

This morning I had a dream. But I have already forgotten. "Yama." "Yama." Hanging to her grandmother's brightly colored skirts. "Watch out for the cars." The rolling cars, with their brightly colored skirts.

That wasn't the way it was, but it was the way it might have been. The roads, long, curved. The roads that curled into the desert. The roads that curled around that patch of land, tying it like a Christmas package with light and warmth and

This morning I had a dream. The bus traveled to the edge of a large, blue lake. Not across roads, but through fields and tall, thin arms of grass.

"Yama," she called, and the call curled around me. "Yama," she called.

Los Angeles is situated in a basin. A flat, grey basin surrounded on four sides by mountains. One of the sides folds down long banks into the sea. Every year or so a part of this fourth wall collapses.

From which direction does the wind flow? It flows from the sea. From which direction does the wind flow? It flows from the sea and into my hands.

San Francisco is water and, crossing the bridge, patterns of lights. Lights suspended on air, on water. And on clear days, rows of hills with houses clutched to their sides. There is a vastness about the land, about the coast. Everything seems too large, unmanageable, like objects to the hands of a small child. The East Coast is different, and New York is cluttered and the distance across the palm of the hand.

Los Angeles, San Francisco, New York. The fourth wall is of an indeterminate size and shape. A desert. An impartial country where the other three are joined together. Every year or so part of this fourth wall collapses.

3.

Clear, the music cries and circles the empty space. Clear and compact like a tightly resolved dance. Like this first afternoon as I wander the streets, as others do, as I see it in their faces also, as I walk. New York. Different as it is now, on this first day of warmth.

Clarity is much to be desired and simplicity is the essence of God. These the words of the Saint. Clarity is much to be desired. Clarity is much... to be...

Whose feet are these that walk along the streets? Whose hands hang down from whose body? These are my feet, my hands, my body. This is my face. The face of the blocks as they pass. In face of the blocks as they pass. In face of these members of my body, my face faces the street. The blocks are passed.

4.

They said it was the best our country had to offer. Of itself, with no intrusion. Behold, here is the land. Behold, here is the school. Behold, here is the fist, bulging, its muscles veined with the gold of the earth.

But it was not the earth of which they spoke. It was the blood of the earth, cut from its body. Los Angeles. Gigantic. Now red. Now purple. Now the Virgin Mary on the boulevard, white and yellow lightbulbs falling from her lips.

I said I did not understand. They said I was young, it was a matter of growth. Of growth. Of learning how to wield the sickle, spread the refuse out, side by side, with the long, uneven rows of grass. When the settlers first came it was a barren country — a desert surrounded by deserts. They brought the stucco and concrete. They brought the horses and the children. They rode over vast ranches of cattle and grain.

This, my father, is what I am. Because one day I stumbled and scarred my knee so that now, twenty years later, I can still see the small white dots standing out against my leg. And after that how hard I found it to walk on your streets.

I took a brush. It was red. I took a brush. It was green, orange, yellow. I took a brush. It was the width of the desert. And into this city I was born and first heard my name.

When you are grown your brush will be red — the color of this city. You will live here, work here, be married here, raise your children here. You will die here.

I will not die in this city. I will not be the color of this desert, cut down the middle with blood.

It was raining when I left and raining when I arrived. The streets, the houses, the color of rain. When I was a child I wanted only two things — I wanted to learn and I wanted to write.

This is the way the lesson goes: in that first city there were shapes, huge and grotesque. In the second there was water, and the land like an arm extended to the sea. The third was built on a rock that could not support its own weight.

There were people. The people that built the city. And there was the fourth...

Long rows of tightly corseted women through the wide, flat streets. Nothing in that hot sun that was not bright, not stripped with color. And the eyes. Always the eyes.

Dressing, speaking, breathing for the eyes.

My father, my mother, my country. The dream that my country provoked in them, in me. This is what you made me. What I am. You gave me eyes and hair. You gave me a body. You sent me out — not as one person, but as a group of people, living under the same skin, gathered together under this union of eyes, hair, body. You gave me a name and you robbed me of that name. You gave me all these things and robbed me of them. But you could not take from me what was never yours to give.

I will not die in your city. I will not be buried under your streets. I will not dress myself in your houses of gold and lies and grotesque forms.

Always you will live here, close as the blood that flows through the veins of my hand. As I walk into the desert.

Father, mother, country. The dream clutched tight to my body, like a lover.

New York, 1964

MORNING POEM

There's always plenty of time
until it runs out on us
But you can't rush things either
They grow at their own speed
reaching for a point of contact
of their own

I am plagued with impatience
inertia
        the two extremes
the edges of everything
Those two things also
being one

Some people build homes   houses
of themselves   I think of Jung
his circular walls
                years of
thought enclosing his body
Trapped in his own ideas

Others travel the streets
planting themselves in their
sidewalks
        Their bodies a motion
more like a dance
And some try both worlds
multiple existences
                are makers of life
Patience is part of it   but more
To have a vision   To make it
real

    Can you see what I'm saying
How time itself is our enemy
our friend   How we trap ourselves
in vision

But how it also opens out
can lead us forward
How we lose things only to find
them again
            Only to find ourselves
different   at the same place

Listen   this morning the world closes
and opens at my fingertips   The sun
is bright   draws me to it
But I sit in a room cluttered with
memories books old pieces of furniture
old pieces of myself

I am inside
            and outside
of it all
I reach out
with what is behind me
I live my death
                am captured
in my life

HOLDING TOGETHER

If you look for me
in the supermarket on Avenue A
on a Saturday morning
                    among green beans
and bananas   rhododendrons
snake plants   swedish ivy
small cans of tuna salmon spam
Do not expect to find me

Do not expect to find me
in the cafeteria on the corner
eating danish
                sipping coffee
staring at the old men
with their long faces and
tired sleeves

or walking filthy summer streets
greeting a neighbor with short
black hair
        matted dog

If you look hard enough
you may find my footsteps
Indentations on walls
                    Faces
my voice has touched
But don't expect to find me
My name scatters itself on
the seasons
        I am hidden
even from myself
In that place of solitude where
poems reside
            and seams

43

CLIPPINGS

History repeats itself
they declare
        wanting us to believe
the present only a duplication
(slightly altered)
            of the past

I sit sorting clippings
scraps of history
        a collage
torn from newspapers   books
fragments of memory
the corners
      of my brain

Who said it first?
How long can you negate what your ears
have heard? How long can you deny
what your eyes have seen?

CLIPPING ONE : a portrait
a woman and a man
their lips drawn tight
You notice first her eyes
           so open
light seems drawn to them
His hand rests against her shoulder
They balance each other
Sean Sands
      brother of dead Irish
hunger striker Bobby
Elizabeth O'Hara   Derry born
and raised

"The violence leaves a mark on all of us,"
she says

A breeze blows gently
outside my window
stirs the single tree
                    In summer
when its leaves are full
the street is hidden
People enter only as sound

Sound is faceless like these words
but it also conveys an image
has dimension   of its own

Sands describes a plastic bullet
4" long 1" in diameter
designed to be fired at the ground
describes 11-year-old Carol Ann Kelly
killed by British soldiers
firing point blank
                    at her face

The cylinder tore her head to bits
It was porcelain hard   The color of cream

The past is a multiplicity of facts
if anything   more obtuse
than the future
                    more liable to alteration
less visible in meaning

but images remain

CLIPPING TWO : an afternoon dispatch
Plastic bullets as well as water cannon
tear gas   armored cars
have now been authorized to control
Britain's own riot-torn streets

At ten Sean Sands is interrogated
his family put out   on the street

Bobby Sands   at gunpoint   is forced
from his job

"That's when he joined the IRA"

My eyes travel across the desk top
CLIPPING THREE : protective raids
(the breaking and entering of private homes)
are now taking place in certain sections
of England
            "to insure the peace"

In all turns back on them on us
as it always does
the violence
            the waste

History belongs to those
who claim it   The past is silent
has only the dimension
                    we place on it
the words we call it
the voice we give it
the power we endow it with
in itself
     it has no name

A lesson forgotten
is a lesson
            never learned

Only those who can see the moments
act on them
            hold them
can alter the past
create history

determine whose future it is
that will be gained

RED

Red means STOP!
It is the color of fire
of passion   revolution
of the sun rising and setting
It is the color of the heart
Flowers are red   & the devil
It is the color of contradiction
of motion   As a child
my chosen favorite was blue
It still is   But I turn to red
as one turns to the future
As one is pulled by the future
to be acknowledged & met

Cuba, Chile, Nicaragua

Jalapa, Nicaragua (on the Honduran border) 1983

In 1972 I spent a month in Chile during the period when Allende was still in power. I met Nicanor Parra and was privileged to see some of the art work of Violeta Parra, a revolutionary Chilean folksinger and composer, whose work I much admire. When I returned home I wrote "First and Last Poems" which represented to me at the time the terrible struggle she had faced confronting the contradictions of being a political woman and artist at a time when there was little support for either. And the subsequent tragedy of her suicide. After Pinochet's fascist coup the poem took on a strange air of premonition and began to symbolize Chile itself to me.

My formal "political education" had really begun in December of 1967 and again in November of 1968 when I traveled to Cuba. I shared a room and friendship with Margaret Randall that first trip taken to attend The Cultural Conference in Havana, an experience having such a profound impact on me that upon returning to the now alien context of New York I found myself quite literally speechless. It was as if I were seeing the city I had lived in for years for the first time. One evening about three weeks after my return I called Margaret in Mexico City where she lived then. Hearing her voice somehow eased the block that had kept me from writing. I sat down immediately after hanging up the phone and wrote the poem "Reminisances" and went on to be able to write and speak in detail about my trip.

The essay "Cuba" was neither written as nor meant to be a thorough analysis and critique of the Cuban situation in the years 1968-69. It was my personal reaction after spending several months there to the contrasts I saw between Cuba and the United States — the hope, the energy, the vision of a society looking toward the future as contrasted to the anger and despair increasingly brought on by the Vietnam War and the reaction of the authorities in the U.S. to dissent and the emerging struggles of national liberation which followed the civil rights movement.

This is not in any way to mitigate the positive feelings I had and have about Cuba but to recognize the often tragic problems that arose during those years in the area of Gay rights. I visited Cuba during a period of relative tolerance of homosexuality, the situation there being little different than in the States at the time and considerably better than some other places in Latin America. I present this essay as it was written and not revised twenty years later because I feel it is important to understand what the vision of a place like Cuba means when you actually experience it.

A dozen years later, in 1983, I would visit Nicaragua to attend a conference on Central America. The essay, "Feminism & The Nicaraguan Revolution" (also unrevised) was written a year after that trip. At that time the Contras had just begun their task of devastating the countryside.

Many of the reforms envisioned and begun by the revolution have now been postponed or destroyed by the long war the Nicaraguans have endured, a war of blood and money, of bullets and blockades. A war which has resulted in a temporary victory by partisans of United States government policy.

It is a testament to the spirit of the revolution that, against overwhelming odds, the struggle continues.

FIRST AND LAST POEMS

for Violeta Parra

there is nothing romantic
about death   about pain
tears falling like soft clouds
like copper clouds   the color of rusted blood
the texture of fire

the first enemy is fear
the second   power
the third   old age

all my life   all those books   all those feelings
words   thoughts   experiences
to say such simple words   to feel
such simple things

your mountains like my own   like home
rows of dust   of light brown soil
as if a gentle wind could level them
could blow them away

the sea   touching my nostrils
filling them   a country of smell
of sound   of wine   flowers   of salt air
of early morning   opening and
opening   through my mind
my heart   the extremities
of my hands   my feet

if I were a bird and could float
dipping and weaving tapestries of air
and light   if we could fly together
like silver crows   birds of dream
until everything stops   is silent and
gentle   like your songs   your voice

but the world allows us nothing
the world is nerves   is fiber
dust and sand   the world changes constantly
nothing remains the same

I see you singing into the air
as if your voice could fly   be free
were there creatures above you
listening   fishing your gifts
from the breeze   was there a place
that could hold you   as you opened yourself
to it   as you went where no one else
could follow   where no one else
could see

    each time I have loved
    I have left part of myself behind
    until now I am mostly memory
    mostly dream   what I have left
    I give to you   my last love
    my last song

    the total of all
    I have ever felt or known

we grow smaller as we grow
as things empty themselves of us
and we of them

it is so deep   this thing between us
no name can contain it
even time trembles at its touch

REMINISCENCES

for Cuba
& for Meg

1
Speaking to you   I was reminded
of those weeks   how far they seem
distant   & yet   how strong

                    speaking to you

    words fail me now   often
    I sit for hours without speech
    images stray through my mind songs

    as I work a feeling of hunger   and then
    of pain

Sometimes   no   often   it is harder to remember and then
on the faces   I discover it   in the streets as I walk
learning to look out   boldly   into those eyes

    it is not despair that turns them away but hope
    you asked why & that is the answer

    refusing solace   refusing their dark places
    their tombs

I sicken of those eyes   their sharp edges   their
wit   I sicken of the sophistication
of those eyes

    by their death   they remind me

    as those others did

                    that winter

so few weeks ago (we spoke together then)

as they did

by their life

2
It is the song that has meaning   I heard them
sing   We heard them   in their winter   Their
hands   their voices   the song   as the poem
its words strong

& behind the words   the meaning   the syllables
the depth

There is this pain inside me   For years now
I have known it   This pain   This companion of
mine

It reduces things cleverly this friend

What is greater than I

it croons to me

it sings to me

What is greater than I

There are things greater   good   good   good

good   What are they

What is more important than this pain

How cleverly it reduces things   this ache
in my side

& those weeks made it deeper   I know now
what caused it   & that it will never leave

56

3
It reminded me   your voice   of those days
The sea outside my window   I could never live long
beyond the reach of sea   At least sensing it there
around me   its song   even its silence   Always
I have lived near water   & there it surrounded me

The East River is not an ocean
Is not beautiful like that sea
Does not break against the streets
furious   & then   calm

But it is water & every now and then a boat passes
& the stillness of it   even the darkness
sometimes

& I see into it as one looks into the water

with the backs of the eye

4
It is not finished   is never over
Repeating again and again   Each time holding
the balance   tipping it
forward

> *The revolution is for people*
> they said   but it was not
> their words

                        it was them

        the way they were   the way they spoke

It was as hard to carry as water

And now months later   I have begun to
live   to speak   the change

the words written in blood   in pain

You could scream it in the streets
and who would listen

But the scream remains   the sound of it
like the sound of your voice   and those
others   like their memory   like water

changing   as it flows

CUBA

In a poem, words are used to achieve an understanding that can only be grasped by the combinations of the words, by their sound, their music, mirroring the full unity of language, the emotion and thought of the poet, the style of the poet's life. All this is a poem. To speak of any element separately is to speak only part of the poem, to understand a part at the expense of the whole. To speak about Cuba, to use words, is always to express only part of the picture, part of the unity, the whole. The best description of the impact of going to Cuba was one I heard on the plane as we were leaving the Havana airport on our return trip. A Norwegian poet I was sitting with said to me: "Before you go to Cuba, it's covered by a blanket of gray. After you land, you leave the grayness behind. There is a clarity about your vision in which the problems as well as the virtues become real." A clarity that extends beyond Cuba to encompass your own life as well.

Cuba is, more than any other place I have ever visited, a country that must be experienced. The question then is how, once having been there, to express the feeling of it, to convey the experience. A list of facts doesn't, can never, do it. The revolution is complete, extending to the most minute levels of human communication. People who had nothing to eat, who could not read or write, who lived without hope, now have education, food, security, a future. For all there is pride, dedication, a sense of humanity. There is almost no illiteracy. Medical service is free. There has been no incidence of polio in four years, a rare phenomenon in Latin America. There are now well over 300,000 students in scholarship schools alone (centered in the former "privileged areas" like Miramar) in an island with a population of under eight million. But there is more. There is the goal toward which all these improvements are centered — and it is a human goal, concerned with human beings.

When I first visited Cuba in 1968, I was attracted by a notice in the newspaper of a puppet theater performance of *The Wizard of Oz*. That was my first contact with the Teatro Guiñol. It impressed me so much that a year later, when I returned to Havana, I made it a point to go to the Teatro Guiñol again. This time they were performing a new play, *Shango de Ima,* one of a series of plays they were working on to bring to the people an understanding and appreciation of Afro-Cuban culture. As they had in *The Wizard of Oz,* the troupe used their ingenuity to the utmost, combining people with puppets, using black light, day-glo paint, a whole range of imaginative techniques, but never using them obtrusively, always with the view of bringing the emotion and meaning of the story into focus. The people and puppets blended together in such a way that any distinction between the two was blurred, any differences obscured and forgotten. The closest comparison I could make is with a Japanese puppet theater I had seen in New York, but in the Teatro Guiñol the puppet holders played a different role — not rigid, not objects or parts of the scenery, they were the puppets themselves, moving when the puppets could not move as the puppets, in their turn, performed in place of the actors.

The imagination demonstrated in the productions of the Teatro Guiñol was a sample of the inventiveness of the artists in Cuba in general, particularly in the fields of literature, theater, graphic arts, and film. My two trips to Cuba differed in the sense that during the first trip, because of my participation in the Cultural Congress in Havana, I was limited in time and concentrated mainly on the cultural aspect of the revolution. My second trip was much longer and gave me a chance to see a great deal of the countryside and the social developments which are part of the revolutionary process. But always, whether the central interest was art or farming or housing, the subject always turned back to one topic, people. That is what the Cuban Revolution is about — people. An affirmation not only of the "rights" of human beings, but human beings themselves.

Altogether, in the over five months I spent in Cuba, I stayed part of the time in Havana, part of the time in the country, where the revolution started and is most in evidence, and in other cities on the island — Santiago de Cuba, Las Villas, Cienfuegos, Santa Clara, the Isle of Youth. I was also privileged to spend two weeks during Christmas with a family in Bayoma, a small town with a long revolutionary history in the province of Oriente. It was in the country side that the rebellion started and it is there that the revolution is most in evidence. The Cubans say that 1959 marked the triumph of the rebellion, but it was just the beginning of the revolution, which is an ongoing process of social change.

San Andres is located almost in the center of Las Villas province. A four-hour drive from Havana, it is perhaps one of the most beautiful valleys in Cuba. But it is much more than the scenery that is important — San Andres is one of the many experimental "integral" communities in Cuba today. In this community of almost five thousand, a community where, before the revolution, there was only one small school, every child is now enrolled in one of the three new schools. There is a communal laundry and kitchen, as well as many new nurseries and day care centers, liberating women from these tasks. Since there is plenty of work and more money than there are things to spend it on, money is secondary and work is done for its own rewards. Most of the extra jobs in the community, in the markets ad other stores, for example, are done on a volunteer basis, since most of the essentials for living are provided without charge. In the schools, the students are housed, fed, and clothed. But more important, they are educated and they take part in a very integral way in the process of education. From an early age they take part in the running and care of their schools, growing their own food, helping to make the schools completely self-sufficient. The school administrators are young — the director of the high school we visited was twenty-four, the teachers averaged between eighteen and twenty-two years. The students have their own libraries, complete infirmaries, nutrition staffs, everything they need. We spend two hours in a fifth-grade class discussing world events with the students, who often caught us off guard with the astuteness of their remarks and the difficulty of their questions. Noticing broken chairs and desks in the junior high, we asked why some of the school equipment was damaged, since the school itself was only two years old. The director explained that it was a result of what they call "pre-revolutionary virus." Most of the older children had never been to school before this school had been built and many of them needed time to adjust to the new situation — they had no idea how to relate to the school and the strange, new equipment. During their process of adjustment some of the property suffered. But property has no value in comparison to people. When we asked about discipline, the director was surprised and said if they punished a child he would hate the school and feel it was a prison. The process of education included the process of establishing relationships, so when they did something destructive, students were talked to about it and it was explained why they should not act that way. And if it happened again, the talk was patiently repeated again and again, by the teachers and — more important — by their peers. In the worst cases the only punishment conceivable was *not* being allowed to work in the fields surrounding the school, which was looked on as a privilege, and having to eat *before* the rest of the children. But, the director said, "Things have improved considerably in the last two years. We are very proud of our school." And he had every right to be.

Cuba. *Territorio Libre*. Free territory of America. Not a freedom of words, of postures, but a freedom of language, of speech. A contagious freedom, it rubs off into your pores, gets into your skin. More than what you hear or see — what you feel. It works itself into you and there you are, suddenly, changed. Not knowing how, or when, or even why it happened.

Driving through the countryside, a military truck passes you in the opposite direction, one of the soldiers playing a Congo drum while other soldiers laugh, sing, dance around him; an old woman in a small room in the Old City of Havana who, upon your question of her reaction and the reaction of her friends to the death of "El Che," begins to cry; flying around a new apartment complex in a bus going at least a hundred miles an hour because there is an extra half-hour and this is something you should see and hanging on with both hands and seeing it.

People. Conversations for hours with people. In all parts of the city. In the country. Sometimes through a friend who speaks Spanish, sometimes through an interpreter, sometimes in English, sometimes in a broken "anti-language" composed of words and

62

phrases in mixed English, Spanish and French. Later, much more fluently, tutored patiently by three old women in my hospital room at the Nacional Hospital, three women liking me, intent on my staying, perhaps I liked the fifteen year old worker down the hall with the broken foot. He would grow up after all. *Muy fuerte.* Or the soldier in the next room. But no, his lungs were bad. One of the best conversations with a poet on the magazine "Bohemia" which consisted mostly of smiling, pointing and sign-language. Two hours one afternoon just to get down one city block. Endless invitations to come in, sit down, accept coffee, rum, and talk.

The Cultural Conference is another story. Like a play within a play. Taking place in Cuba and permeated with the enthusiasm, the spirit of Cuba, yet in itself a unit, comprised of over five hundred people from almost every country in the world. The stated purpose of the conference was to talk about the problem of culture in the Third World. I say "stated purpose" because not only was the central topic thoroughly discussed, but many other areas were also opened up for discussion and action. The conference was divided into five commissions: one political, one on the formation of the "new human," one of the responsibility of the intellectual to the underdeveloped nations, one on mass media, and one on science and technology. The Cubans, in order to avoid charges of "stacking" the conference kept their own delegations intentionally small. To avoid trying to divide my time between all five commissions, which might end with my not understanding any of them, I decided to follow one commission through from beginning to end. And since I had a number of friends in the third commission, I decided to attend the second, the one that interested me the most, the formation of the "new human."

There were about 100 people in the second commission. Papers were presented to the chairman, and each paper was read and discussed. Among the delegates were Hans Magnus Enzenberger, a poet from West German; David Cooper, a psychiatrist from London; Robert Matta, a Chilean painter; Alain Jouffroy, a French poet, and, sitting next to me, a physical education instructor from Cuba, a teacher from Guinea, a track star from Czechoslovakia, a painter from France, a philosopher from Belgium, and a poet from North Vietnam.

The idea of the "new human" is based on Marx's original conception of the development of a new type of human being in a society in which community is a living fact rather than an ideal, and brought up to date by Che Guevara in his writing on the twenty-first century person...a new human being with a new technology. It is "not a question of how many kilograms of meat are eaten or how many pretty imported things can be bought with present wages. It is rather that the individual feels greater fulfillment, that he has greater inner wealth and many more responsibilities." This is Che — his idea of the new human. "Let me say, with the risk of appearing ridiculous, that the true revolutionary is guided by strong feelings of love. It is impossible to think of an authentic revolutionary without this quality." Che — himself the "new human." "To achieve complete spiritual recreation in the presence of his own work, without the direct pressure of the social environment but bound to it by new habits." The new human, the new society. A whole society, without arbitrary divisions between worker, soldier, intellectual, artist. Practical as well as theoretical, already in process, already begun. I talked about art and about education and was asked immediately how I would apply my ideas to children, to youth, to older people and if I had a practicable system worked out. Not enough to know what you want to do, the question is *how*, how do you do it.

Matta got up and spoke about rain, and being young, and paint, and the rooftops in Chile: "It is not a question of just backing the Revolution; it is a question of being revolutionary. And being revolutionary implies, of course, being free or consequently struggling to achieve freedom... A revelation must take place, all the possibilities of man should be made evident..." Matta, speaking about the "internal guerrilla," living his words as he speaks them. Papers on education, on revolution, on the rights of women, of the problems of youth, lines from Wilhelm Reich, arguments, debates. Endless hours of discussion. Not empty words — words to be taken in and lived.

The general resolution of the conference was a strong one — condemnation of the war in Vietnam, support for revolution and the "new human." But the sum total of the conference, its strength, could never be expressed in a few pages of prose. In all there were over three hundred papers delivered and hours of discussion and debate. The third commission — the responsibility of intellectuals to the third world — drafted a resolution that was overwhelmingly supported by the conference delegates, a resolution that no longer would any of these artists, philosophers, scientists, teachers, take money from any foundation or government, publish in or lend their names to any institution actively supporting the deprivation of the people of the third world.

Sitting one afternoon in the lobby of the hotel, I began talking to a poet from North Vietnam. Upon hearing I was a poet from New York, he jumped up. "Wait here, I have something to show you." He came back with a book of poems, his favorite: Walt Whitman, in French, bent, dog-eared. With it was a poem he had written for a Cuban newspaper about Whitman and about Vietnam — about Vietnam and about the love of the Vietnamese people for Whitman, for his ideal, for their ideal, which was the same. Poetry which was for them a living force.

Cuba changes you. The Cubans are trying to work out a society of affirmation and revolution in its profoundest aspects and the change is subtle and lasting. This is not to say there are no problems. The economic blockade and the continuing active hostility of the United States government has caused many material shortages and is a continuing presence. But the goal of trying to create a new kind of society, of trying to overcome underdevelopment, of trying to maintain a true revolutionary situation would be difficult under any circumstances. The problems are many and as great as the task that has been set. "The novelty of revolutionary thinking lies precisely in the fact that it does not pretend to be infallible; in that it is defined as a continuous creation and boldness, and in that it is a matter of limiting as much as possible the margin of error giving proofs of courage and facing the risks to be run," Alain Jouffroy said. And it is true. The problems are many. The problems of creation and change. But perhaps change is the wrong word. In Cuba you catch a glimpse of the future and that glimpse strengthens you for your own work. A revolution must be a revolution for all people, freedom for everyone. Until the last person on earth is free, no one can be free.

That is the lesson of the Cuban Revolution. Not guilt, but work. Not a choice, but a work. Working as individuals, as groups so that these groups, these individuals, can come together and create through their own separate works, a great work. The poem is never empty of meaning, of reason, of life. The dream becomes real and being real can be dealt with with anger and with love.

Havana, 1968
New York, 1969

LETTER FROM HAVANA

for René Vallejo Ortiz

1.

Always I have found it easier to write in the form of a letter, to imagine I am writing to someone, to have a specific person in mind, a specific idea I am trying to express. To piece together, word by word, a motive, a reaction, a part of my life. As though my hands were that half-way point between my thoughts and my heart.

And so I am writing this, this letter. Trying to explain a little this one day, or the series of days that make up this letter, this piece of my life. As I begin now, in the month of December, 1968, in the city of Havana, so few and yet so many miles from my home.

2.

Home. How many homes. In how many cities. Like the lines of a poem, spreading across a continent and beyond, woven as one, to form one body, one thought. So many places and yet always that one place. Where we are at each precise moment, at each second of time.

It is always hardest to begin. To know where, to know how, to begin. Silent, thoughts flow easily, but now, at this desk, it is hard. There was a time, once, two years ago or more, when time took a different direction. Explaining at the same time so much and yet so little. How it was possible and how I came to be in that place, in the midst of it. Time. Not as we know it, but at another place. As it is. And yet I know now that too was another dream. How much closer and still how far away.

This is not clear. But some things are not said so easily. Are not simple sentences. Are not phrases that come easily to words. Are not of words. But leave behind a level of truth that knows, that feels, that is.

And where is it now? That thing that was felt so deeply. Felt And then gone. As time passes and we pass with it, leaving behind? A sadness. And a need.

3.

We build models mimicking our own form. A camera, a pair of eyes. A tool, an extension of the hand. The connections of our own body. And now our minds...

But that experience. That moment in time. Did it have anything to do with me? What part of me was in it? What was it? What was it I have known — that continues to haunt me, that sets me apart?

(July 10, 1939. 12:15 P.M. Philadelphia — a place, a time, a date.)

He read it wrong, so wrong — forgetting, or never having learned, that revolution, revelation was the key. Pluto, the patience, the will, the steady and inevitable change.

"We solve today's problems, today" — another voice. This one close, sure, and there too a loneliness beyond death. Beyond my comprehension. Because when others die, that is the pain too great. Pain and knowledge — those two things that set one apart.

Backwards into the future, like passengers on a train, we ride forward, our faces toward the past.

Cancer: water. Libra: the balance. Aries: fire. And always there, like a fist, Aquarius, alone, red, angry, a square of death. A square of love.

Has it happened before, in other ways, in another time, and I, who am so impatient, waiting, forced now to wait. Because there are things that cannot be pushed. Can only be prepared for, fought for, lived for.

To prepare, to fight, and to wait.

4.

It is another day now. Another of many days. And something new has entered since that time. Because it was not enough to know, because that knowledge must now be transformed, because it is this earth we live on, and apart from ourselves are others who also wait, whose need is greater, because for them not even the first step exists.

It was this I had to learn, that I now know. It was this I learned in a way, last year, one year ago, in this same city, in a way that cannot be erased, that was real, as that other experience also was real. That without those others, nothing exists. Because we do not live in a world apart. Only our death is ours alone, and that only as experience, not as fact.

Because we die as we live, with those others, or we do not live or die at all.

5.
We are condemned to light. And that is the truth of it. And it is now that we begin, together, knowing a certain end. For all of us, together, or for none of us at all.

6.
A poem must be written to someone, cannot be created of air, delivered to the wind. And so I write to you, in these sentences, long, broken, whatever it takes to express, but never expresses fully, what it is I must say.

One sentence to say it all. One word. But what is it? Years. And still that cannot be reached.

"We must always remember the complexity of the simple." In a book, somewhere, those words, that ritual, that complex of words, of dance, of song. I fight my own doubt, knowing now, after these years, what is there, fight by own doubt, my eyes, how I see, my hands, how they write, my body, my mind, how it feels, how it sees. Knowing this other, not beyond, but within, as part, all, another way. No longer the pieces, but the whole. Death has many faces. They say a person sees many things before they die, that their life passes before their eyes, that they know what has passed and what is to come.

I thought tonight as I sat, the room turning before my eyes, that I must have died many times. As I saw it turn, that life, before my eyes. I can no longer use the words, must talk to them, must let them talk to me, tell me what they mean.

As they come from other mouths. As I find them on other pages. As I find myself no longer alone.

Havana, Cuba
Winter, 1969

FEMINISM &
THE NICARAGUAN REVOLUTION

1. Nicaragua: Being There

Knowing something intellectually, even physically situating yourself in a particular location, and "being there" are very different experiences. Statistics, facts, history, analysis, theory are absolutely essential in understanding what is happening today in Nicaragua, why it is happening and what it means to us as women in the United States. But there is a sense of the country, the people a context that must be transmitted for these facts to come to life. In Spanish two distinct words are used to express simplicity — *simple* and *sencillo*. While *simple* is translated as easy, superficial, simple-minded, silly, *sencillo* — its deepest meaning untranslatable — means direct, unadorned, unpretentious, stripped bare. *Sencillo* is a word you hear over and over in Nicaragua, a word that becomes riveted in your mind, that becomes a kind of cipher, a kind of key, not only to the Nicaraguan experience, but to your own vision, your own perception of the world around you, your own society as well as theirs.

As Americans coming from an industrialized, technological society that equates complexity with progress and profundity, importance with size, that educates through image and representation rather than direct experience — whether in the university or through movies or T.V. — it is most easy for us to miss the obvious, to overlook what is right in front of our eyes. One of the things that struck me most coming home from Nicaragua was the consciousness of so many people literally plugged into some mechanical device, not looking at real things but at images of things. Not perceiving, knowing directly, losing individual judgment, choice. Learn it through T.V., through someone else's ears, voice. People, instead of relating to each other, enticed into relating to a re-presentation — not the event, but the recreation of the event — even finally electing a movie star to act out being

71

president. Writing this, it seems "simple" enough, even simplistic, but when you directly confront it after being in a country like Nicaragua, the contrast is overwhelming.

This should not be misconstrued as a romanticization of "under-development." After all, one of the first things the Nicaraguans did was to send out literacy brigades, mostly quite young people, 60% women,[1] in a successful campaign to reduce the illiteracy rate to 12% from a figure over 50%[2] — the estimated illiteracy among women was much higher than that, rumors even place the figure over 80%. Illiteracy — the inability to generalize, the inability to carry over skills learned in one area to another area (for example, how to stop planting sugar cane and start diversifying crops.)[3] It means a population unable to participate fully in the political process. Ironically, of course, even though illiteracy has been traditionally thought of in relationship to under-development, many people in the United States are now to a large extent functionally illiterate — and that is true in every social class. *Sencillo* does not mean one-dimensional or easy, it is extremely difficult — both to understand and to express.

Because behind these words, the facts, the theory, is the actual experience of being in Nicaragua. Beyond all this, for me, being in Nicaragua was actually confronting the faces of the young/old children in the border town of Jalapa, scene of fighting and death where militia and army now outnumber the town's small population. It was to step on the miles of grassy waste that were once central Managua, never rebuilt — the millions of dollars of foreign aid and contributions to do so squandered by Somoza and his National Guard. Nicaragua was the bullet holes riddling the front window of an old pick-up truck loaded with corn; a young woman singing the songs of Victor Jara at 7 o'clock in the morning on the front steps of her house in Ocotal in the war zone two hours from the border, also scene of recent intense fighting; the poems of a boy not more than 10 years old, neck circled by a red F.S.L.N. scarf, reciting at a Christian base community meeting in León; a ceremony on the Honduran border honoring a regiment that had just spent six months fighting often hand-to-hand with the

"Todos Las Armas Al Pueblo: (All Arms to the People).
Mothers of slain children at a military ceremony in Jalapa, July 1983

Jalapa, Nicaragua

In honor of the 4th Anniversary celebration; Jalapa, Nicaragua "contras" (counter-revolutionaries), on the speakers' platform mothers who had lost their children in the struggle.

For me, Nicaragua was the endless discussion, endless work, lasting long into the night — nights of three and four hours sleep, a common occurrence there. It was the tin and clapboard houses of *Ciudad Sandino* and much of the "temporary" housing put up to shelter over 150,000 left homeless in the earthquake of 1972 juxtaposed with the swimming pools and lavish lawns of the now-ousted Somocistas. It was the hot, hot sun and the sheets of sudden rain, and a total change in the sense of scale you are used to. It is smaller, closer, less. It is the directness in things that can't be counted or touched.

For a North American, to travel to Nicaragua is to learn your own history as well as theirs — the two so closely, so violently intertwined. It is to be thrown back on yourself, to learn your own contradictions, strengths, responsibilities. To really "see" Nicaragua demands this kind of dialogue, struggle—both internal and external on every level. "Being there" is more than a physical presence, it is an emotional and intellectual commitment. I think I began first to understand that concretely one night at a Christian base community, after two hours on the road, hot, dirty, late, hungry, trying to figure out what I was doing in what looked like an outdoor high school basketball court (which I think it was), in what was basically a small group of Nicaraguans; trying to understand what was really going on as one by one they got up, sang, recited a poem; trying to talk to the woman sitting next to me, her children; trying for a moment at least to put myself, my notions, my pre-conceptions aside. As Margaret Randall put it when I wrote her on my return to New York:

(What you say) is...so *hard* to get across to most people from the more industrialized societies whose natural sophistication have taken them to a plane both beneficial and preventing their contact often with what is most important, most real, most true...how complicated we have been trained to make it, in the U.S. to keep us from seeing *what's really happening.*[4]

Not just in Nicaragua, but perhaps most important, here, to ourselves, in our own search as feminists, as women.

75

2. Mass Organizations, Liberation Theology & the Movement of Women

Women's participation in the Nicaraguan revolution is certainly unprecedented in the history of revolutionary movements to this date, both in terms of numbers and importance. In fact, it is estimated that by the final offensive of the revolution, "women made up an estimated 30% of the Sandinista army and held important leadership positions, commanding everything from small units to full battalions. In the crucial final battle of León, four out of seven commanders of that military front were women."[5]

This was a result of several factors at least: the continuing struggle of the worldwide women's movement — Dora Maria Tellez relates that one of the ten books available to F.S.L.N. cadre underground was Margaret Randall's *Cuban Women Now*[6]; conditions within Nicaragua itself — according to Lea Guido, Minister of Health and head of AMPRONAC, the women's organization that preceded AMNLAE,

> ...a key factor in the unprecedented participation of women of popular sectors is their role as the economic pillar of the family in Nicaragua. As many as 50% of the households are headed by single women abandoned by men who fathered their children. Even when the men remain with their families, the high rate of both seasonal and permanent unemployment has hinged family survival on the ingenuity and industriousness of women.[7]

Additionally, the emphasis on "prolonged peoples' warfare" and thereby on mass organizations "in all sectors and at all levels under a multiplicity of tactics and organizational forms that could speak to a multiplicity of contradictions,"[8] and certainly the realization of what happened in Chile where the needs of women and their place in the struggle were, if not totally ignored certainly not emphasized, led to the founding of AMPRONAC and its development as a strong and integral part of the struggle.

Although it would be a tremendous mistake to underestimate the influence of traditional Marxist thought, the ability of the Nicaraguans to consolidate a struggle with the broadest possible ideological base — within the limits of those actually interested in social change — is an instrumental factor. This can be seen in relationship to both sexism and racism. Sexism and racism are seen as phenomena in their own right that have to be dealt with ideologically as well as legislated in everyday practice. In the October 24, "International Barricada" the international edition of the F.S.L.N. newspaper, Angela Rosa Acevedo, representing AMNLAE, noted at the Fifteenth Latin American Sociology Congress that "not everything has been resolved for Nicaraguan women..."

> machismo is a part of the historical legacy of a society based on exploitation and still persists in many men and women.[9]

Many women joined the Sandinistas because of the freedom for women relative to their normal lives under Somoza. Certainly this in itself would be an interesting comparison with the position of women historically in the left in this country.

To foreigners at least the analysis of oppression in Nicaragua more often is spoken of in terms of imperialism rather than internal class struggle as a primary modus operandi. Not that class struggle is not seen as operative or casual inside Nicaragua, to the contrary, but the history of Nicaragua has to be analyzed first in terms of external causal relationships. A concrete analysis of imperialism in this perspective shows why the triumph against Somoza in 1979 would be the beginning rather than the culmination of the revolutionary process — a process further complicated by continuing external pressures exerted by former Somocistas outside Nicaragua in league with sympathizers from the middle class and the powerful support and instigation of the United States. Nicaraguans, as a result of neo-colonialism, have been and continue to be the butt of both racism and sexism and this is a further reason why both forms of discrimination are discussed both in traditional Marxist terms and as phenomena on their own.

Another leg of this "poly-theoretical" base is found in the amalgamation of Christianity and Marxism. It is essential to remember that most Nicaraguans are Catholic and Catholicism permeates every facet of their life and thought. Political and religious beliefs are inter-related in Nicaragua in a way that is hard for us in the United States to grasp. Certainly one thing that surprises visitors to Nicaragua is the extent of deep religious involvement there, including the on-going struggle between the traditional church and "liberation theology." The religious underpinnings of the Nicaraguan revolution is an issue that with few exceptions is either completely ignored in the establishment media here or terribly distorted. It has to be, because you can't claim the Nicaraguan government as Marxist/Soviet/Atheist and use that to scare people, and at the same time say Miguel D'Escoto, the equivalent of our Secretary of State, is a Catholic priest, that the Minister of Culture, Ernesto Cardenal, is a Catholic priest. In fact, to hear D'Escoto speak is to hear a speech whose images are those of the New Testament and the Christian religion. He freely uses images of incarnation and religious commitment. This attitude was best summed up one night at dinner when he said, for the Nicaraguan revolution, "being more" was not having more, but giving and loving more.[10]

While it is impossible to understand the present negative status of abortion legislation without understanding the impact of Catholicism in Nicaragua, it is also necessary to take into account the tremendous positive political effects of the Christian base communities which were responsible for bringing so many into the struggle. As Norma Galo remembers:

> Luckily, back in Managua, a priest came to our neighborhood who fit his parish just like a ring on a finger. He felt uneasy knowing the barbarities all around us, and he and we organized our Christian base community, which he said had to be born from our needs. In fact, we first learned to define our needs. Our people did not know how to speak out in public. It terrified them to stand in the priest's place and read from the Bible. But the priest pushed us to learn to express ourselves, and our Christian base community came to mean for us the most open place, the place where we poor really had a voice. Once we could articulate the extremity of our oppression, we realized we were not doing enough as Christians to fight it.[11]

Two excellent books on liberation theology are Penny Lernoux's *Cry of the People* and Margaret Randall's, *Christians in the Nicaraguan Revolution.*

This is not to imply that Nicaragua is a dream world, a utopia, and that a revolution is an instant fix for centuries of problems. A pitfall we all too often slip into. One that insures disillusionment.

Nicaragua today is involved in a revolutionary process, a profound process of social change, a process which is trying to be inclusive rather than exclusive. The relationship between social classes, sexual relationships, individuals' consciousness of themselves as part of a community is being irrevocably altered. Everything is being called into question and discussed and discussed and discussed and this in an atmosphere of present and imminent war.

Revolution by its nature frees contradictions that have been buried and ignored — all the anger, frustration, prejudice, along with the tenacity, courage and sacrifice. The problem of sexism is far from being solved or, in some cases, even identified. Mistakes have been made and no doubt in the future will continue to be made. The Nicaraguans would be the first to acknowledge this, to be surprised that anyone could realistically imagine differently. Revolution to them is not an abstraction. It is the concrete actions of specific human beings. It is a human thing.

3. Women & the Nicaraguan Revolution

Women in Nicaragua took part on every level of revolutionary activity from support positions to leadership positions, including comandantes fighting in the field. They continue to be the backbone of the Nicaraguan revolution and hold leadership positions in many revolutionary institutions. But the struggle against "machismo" has just begun.

Although AMNLAE is the mass women's organization and presently has a current membership of 50,000,[12] there are many other organizations in which women take a major role — including the important CDS.

Women to be found in top leadership positions are Lea Guido, Daisy Zamora, Nora Astorga in the Revolutionary Government; Commander Doris Tijerino, Commander Olga Aviles, Sub-Commander Eleonora Rocha and Sub-Commander Julia Guido in the Armed Forces; and on the F.S.L.N. Board of Directors, Commander Letica Herrera and Commander Dora Maria Tellez. 47% of all Nicaraguan women are in the militia and seven Reserve Battalions of the Sandinista Popular Militia are made up entirely of women.[13] Within recent months, because of the military crisis in Nicaragua, active recruitment has begun of women into the regular army — a move that was not anticipated until next year at the earliest.[14]

Leo Guido, Minister of Public Health and Secretary General of the women's organization during its years of struggle against Somoza, addressed the conference on Central America in Managua in July,1983,[15] on the gains in health care and education under the revolutionary government — the eradication of polio, the improvement of the infant mortality rate (one of the highest in Latin America going in four years from 121 dead per thousand born alive under Somoza to 88 per thousand today), the inroads against gastroenteritis, which was one of the chief killers in a country whose average life expectancy was 53 years old — 20 years less than the United States — a country where 50% of deaths occurred before 14 years of age.

Guido emphasized that the peoples' political consciousness was not a result of some "exotic theory, but of experience," that it was a consciousness formed by oppression and exploitation. She explained that the Sandinista victory was a result of the organization of women, of farmers, of labor unions — a broad band of organizations which gave everyone a place. "This explains a victory that is impossible to explain in terms of military training and weapons." She stated that the substantial changes that have occurred since the revolution regarding the role and place of women in Nicaragua have

> taken place through the struggle, when women joined the revolution massively and assumed all the tasks. When the comrades had to accept the fact that women had the same or more capacity to face the task. This place has been won by us.

Furthermore, she continued (when asked specifically about relations between men and women) that men cannot be liberated when their relationship to women is that of master to slave. The liberation of women, for Guido, is defined in multiple ways — in terms of specific relationships, in economic terms, in political terms — simply knowing *and* doing:

> ...the simplest woman in the fields, in the markets, is now able to tell you the problems we have regarding supplies in the field of health,

everything, the problems in defense. She can talk to you about foreign policy. She is aware of many problems that in the past were only known by a few or by men. Today, men as well as women can talk and implement the things they learn and see. There is a clear policy of fighting against that situation of domination and exploitation women have lived in. But we are aware that the situation faced by women does not change only through the theory of feminine struggle, but by changing the living conditions of a people.

Relating to conditions women face having to care for their children, earn a living, as well as take part in direct political struggle, Guido stated that in spite of all the problems being faced by Nicaragua today, and the inordinate amount of the small monies they have available having to be spent on defense, they have not closed any hospitals or day care centers where working women leave their children, and the cultural events, CDS committees, militias which provide the possibilities for community action are being expanded. She concluded her remarks with the statement, "We cannot say *machismo* has disappeared, but we have only had four years when you put it next to a century of exploitation."

While it is obvious from this last statement that Lea Guido is working from a theoretical analysis of *machismo* based on "economic exploitation" rather than "patriarchal exploitation" *per se,* there is a clear understanding of what the effects of *machismo* are, and a fundamental push to correct conditions that will enable women who might not otherwise have the opportunity to participate politically, to change their society in line with their needs.

Some important laws directly concerning women have already been passed by the revolutionary government. "The Statute on Rights and Guarantees" was passed by the Governmental junta for National Reconstruction in August, 1979, the first year of the revolution. It "guarantees the equality of every citizen before the law without regard to birth, race, color, sex, language, opinions, origin, economic condition or any other social condition" and furthermore guarantees "equality within the family in which spouses have equal rights." The statute also makes clear that it is the *obligation* of the government "to remove by every available means the obstacles which impede in practice the equality of citizens and their participation in the political, economic and social life of the country."[16]

There is also "The Law of Communication Media" which prohibits the commercialization of women and "forbids the use of a woman's image as a sex object for advertising."

Some of the changes in the "Law on Social Security" that directly affect women are the reduction of maternity leave time to four weeks before birth along with the extension of leave time after birth to eight weeks. Equal promotion opportunities for all with no other limitations than those of time of service and capacity, breaks, free time opportunities, reasonable limitation of work hours and periodic paid vacations of sufficient length as well as paid holidays are also provided in this law.

Another important law is the "Law of Nature" which makes the father equally responsible, both economically and psychologically, "in regard to material needs, care, education, affection, etc. within the family" with the mother and "explicitly recognizes the social value of domestic work." This applies *regardless* of the marital status of the man and woman.

One way direct participation in government is evidenced is in laws being published and passed out for general discussion and possible change by the people. One famous incident that relates to this procedure was the recent discussion and unprecedented vote in the Council of State — the deliberative body — by AMNLAE, the women's organization, who voted *against* the new draft law on the grounds that it discriminated against women by *not* making draft mandatory for women. The issue was debated by representatives from AMNLAE for a full day and a booklet explaining the position was published.

In regard to homosexuality, while it is a subject not explicitly dealt with on the level other subjects are discussed, "There is no marginalization of gays in Nicaragua...and the subject is discussed in the Party (thus far with a great deal of maturity, there are gays in important party positions.)"[17]

While birth control in Nicaragua is now not only legal, but is provided free of charge in health clinics, abortion is still illegal. Even though in a large public gathering if you ask about abortion people might act as if they didn't hear the question, the problem is being recognized and dealt with. This particular issue is addressed in an interview Margaret Randall did with Milú Vargas, the chief legal counsel for the Council of State,[18] who replies to the question of whether she thinks the present laws against abortion will change by first explaining that under present law — a law passed *before* the revolutionary government took power — a woman can only have an abortion if her life is in danger, and worse, consent must be given by the man, not the woman. "And it is your (the woman's) body, and it is your life that is being toyed with." She goes on to say that she became actively involved in this question after finding out the number of women in Managua who are admitted to hospitals yearly because of illegal abortions and states that the number of reported abortions in Managua is about 5,000 a month "and that only in Managua, and those only reported."

She concludes her comments by saying:

> I think it is necessary to respond to this situation sooner than later. But we are in this situation of imminent war, and we cannot just proclaim a law on abortion without preparing people. Because there is going to be controversy. We can't just proclaim this law without a base. I think that the first step, as women, or better yet, for the organization representing women, is to start dealing with this topic and discussing it.

AMNLAE has already started sex education discussion groups for women on all educational levels, including adult study groups that were an outgrowth of the literacy campaign. For women that aren't covered in any other way, meetings are held in health clinics. These discussion groups enable women to begin to verbalize their feelings and needs and raise consciousness around issues like abortion.

One of the other things that AMNLAE is doing now is sponsoring over 300 garden collectives to teach nutrition — bringing vegetables into the diet and even teaching how to make tofu and milk from soy beans. These collectives also allow women to own land who have never had that right before.

Another mass organization in which women play a major role is the CDS, which perhaps more than any other group has been maligned in this country. The block committees, besides self-defense duties — almost 90% of those doing self-defense patrol are women — have other extremely important functions in terms of neighborhood organizing, doing everything from making sure everyone has ration cards to supervising vaccinations.

Norma Galo relates:

> People in this neighborhood do revolutionary vigilance with the CDS. They watch what's going on in the streets 24 hours a day. If they see some man hitting a woman, he will go to jail and lose his job, too. In the early days of doing revolutionary vigilance, we did surprise some men hitting their wives and we drove the men out of their houses and to jail. And we taught the women about their rights. Some were farm women who had not learned to read yet and who had been brought to the city by men who wanted a dependent, submissive woman. We'd say to these women, "You can't let yourself be hit because on July 19th we women won our full rights." An incident like this happened right in front of my own house. I grabbed the man by his shirt and stopped him even though he screamed in protest. The police took him to prison. Next day I talked to the woman and said, "Look, this guy's no good for you. He's hit you a lot. You're really young, and you can find another man. This one isn't worth it." Later we found out that he had another wife.[19]

The CDSs obviously also function as support groups for women, in the midst of a social change that is shaking apart many lives. Kimiko Hahn relates a particularly poignant story about an experience her group had with a CDS in *Ciudad Sandino*:

> Then, they didn't have guns, they had sticks and whistles. We went out walking in the streets, and they didn't know we were coming because the place we were to visit was chosen randomly. They blew the whistle on us! We explained who we were and they were very gracious and told us all sorts of stories. We asked if they had done this during Somoza's time and they answered. "Are you kidding — we couldn't ever sit outside when he was in power!" If children walked down the street, the National Guard would check their elbows and knees for bruises and scratches which would presumably indicate they'd received Sandinista training. If they had bruises, they were taken to a pit, lined up at the top and someone in the trees would machine-gun them down. You could not even dare look for the bodies.[20]

The Nicaraguans are trying to work out their revolution in the midst of a history of exploitation and poverty and a present of increased U.S. economic and military pressure. There is always the danger that after the revolution "settles in" the movement of women will be reversed. That happened to some degree during the early stages of the triumph over Somoza when the pressure eased off slightly. But never in the history of revolution so far, because of all the various factors mentioned, have women taken so major a role. It would not be an exaggeration to say that at the grass roots level, finally, by the end of the revolution, perhaps the major role. There are no women in the nine-person junta — the reason given is that it is composed of the three top people in each of the three major tendencies in the F.S.L.N. But whatever the reason there are still no women. There is obviously a long way to go, but the road the Nicaraguans are carving speaks for itself. The Nicaraguan revolution is in danger now, and that danger also threatens women in the United States. The Nicaraguan model is not a literal one, the circumstances in Nicaragua are quite different than here, but it is a model of strong and determined women who are working together, from all social classes and interests, to form a new society.

Dora Marie Tellez, one of the comandantes who led the victory in León said in an interview with *Granma:*

> ...the Nicaraguan revolution has had the largest participation of women because it is the most recent. In the next revolution, no matter where it happens, there are going to be more women...The Latin American woman has awoken.[21]

These are words, and words can be deceptive. To be in Nicaragua is to feel the strength of the women, their determination, their spirit, their will. Perhaps the relationship of the experience of "being there" for a North American feminist to our own struggle is summed up best by Adrienne Rich, who also attended the Conference on Central America:

> We have to assume that people do change, that feminism is changing, that socialism is changing, that the liberation movements will teach and learn from one another...I want to suggest that United States feminism has a peculiar capacity to break out of the nightmare and place itself more intelligently with other liberation movements (often led by women from whom we have much to learn) because the spiritual and moral vision of the United States' women's movement is increasingly being shaped by women of color. The concepts of identity

politics, of simultaneity of oppressions, of concrete experience as a touchstone for ideology, the refusal to accept "a room of one's own" in exchange for not threatening the system — these have been explored, expanded on, given voice, most articulately by women of color, and to say this is not to set up competitions or divisions, but to acknowledge a precious resource, along with an indebtedness, that we can all share.[22]

The Nicaraguan revolution has meaning for us *not only* because of what is happening in Nicaragua but because of what is happening in the feminist movement here in the United States.

But as I write these words each day carries more news of incursions into Nicaraguan territory — the bombing of oil resources, rape, murder, the burning of houses, kidnappings, the rumors of imminent massive attack, this time by "contras" backed up not only by Honduran troops, but by thousands of American troops and a flotilla of American warships. And I can't help thinking of my journey to Jalapa and Ocotal and the Nicaraguans we had met and grown so close to in that brief but intense visit, and Margaret and the faces of women indelibly etched in my mind and that word, *sencillo* — simple, but far from easy, the farthest thing from easy to live or to express. The Nicaraguan programme is being carried out by human beings with all the contradictions that human nature entails. It is a difficult programme even under the best of circumstances. Its implications for women are explicit, concrete. I came away from Nicaragua more than ever convinced, more conscious of the fact that our struggle as women, as human beings, and the struggle of the Nicaraguans is the same struggle, against the same oppressive forces, both internal and external. I came back from Nicaragua angry and depressed by my country's actions in Central America, the suffering that was being carried out in my name. I came back from Nicaragua energized, sharing with Adrienne the necessity of defending the hope of that revolution, the fragility and strength of it:

...what most entered my heart and soul, in that brief time of being in the physical presence of a revolutionary process, was the quality I think we are all here tonight trying to affirm — Hope. The sense that it can change. We ourselves can change it.[23]

That the only way change is possible is to *actively* assume as one of our priorities stopping what our government is doing in Central America, as well as all other parts of the world, as *part* of our feminist struggle. That only in that way is any true dialogue between us possible.

FOOTNOTES

1. Margaret Randall, "Conversando con la compañera Milu Vargas, " trans. Susan Sherman. unpublished, p. 2.
2. Guido, taped translation, July 15, 1983.
3. Information taken from a conversation with Edmundo Desnoes, Havana, Cuba, 1968 on the subject of illiteracy and underdevelopment.
4. Margaret Randall, "Letter to Susan Sherman," September 17, 1983. unpublished.
5. Norma Stoltz Chincilla, "Women in Revolutionary Movements: The Case of Nicaragua," *Revolution in Central America*, p. 431. An excellent article to set the context of the position of women in Nicaragua — historically and at the present time.
6. Patricia Flynn, "Women Challenge the Myth," *NACLA: Report on the Americas*, Vol.XIV, no.5, Sept.-Oct., 1980, p. 29.
7. Patricia Flynn, "Women Challenge the Myth," pp. 29-30.
8. Norma Stoltz Chincilla, "Women in Revolutionary Movements," p. 425.
9. "A Committed Sociology," *Barricada Internacional*, Vol.I:II, No.86, Monday, October 24, 1983.
10. Kimiko Hahn, *et al.* "Nicaraguan Dialogue, " *Womanews*, December, 1983.
11. Norma Gallo "Communism, Religion and War," *Voices from Nicaragua*, Vol.1, No. 2-3, p. 7
12. Xeroxed handout from AMNLAE, "untitled," unpublished, p. 1.
13. *Ibid.*, pp. 1-2.
14. Magda Enriquez, informal talk, unpublished, November, 1983.
15. Guido, taped translation, July 15, 1983.
16. Xeroxed handout from AMNLAE, p. 3. Milu Vargas Interview, p. 7.

17. Margaret Randall, "Letter to Susan Sherman," p. 1.
18. Milú Vargas Interview, pp. 10-11. The rest of the remarks in this paragraph are from the same interview.
19. Norma Galo, *Voices from Nicaragua*, p. 10.
20. Kimiko Hahn, *et al.*, "Nicaraguan Dialogue."
21. Norma Stoltz Chincilla, *Revolution in Central America*, p. 426.
22. Adrienne Rich, Speech delivered at "Women in Struggle: Seneca, Medgar Evers, Nicaragua" evening sponsored by IKON magazine, October 28, 1983. *Womanews*, December, 1983.
23. *Ibid.*

FROM NICARAGUA A GIFT

for Margaret Randall

If you were to ask me
to name a color for that land
I would say it was green
But the color you sent was yellow
A plane descending into green
The sun rising golden beyond its wings

Many things are made of gold
A voice sometimes is known as golden
A wedding ring
      Even silence
(when chosen)

But "to be silenced"
That's a different matter
That's to choke on one's own words
erupt in violence
      an act of war

Margaret   today   in your letter
folded in a press release
COVERT ACTIONS AGAINST NICARAGUA
CHALLENGED BY INTERNATIONAL LAW
a small shard of foil falls out
slips to the floor
      I can't make it out
It puzzles me
What is it?   What does it say?
A rectangular shape   in the center
a golden face
circled by yellow   edged by red
 — a cigar band —
      a cigar band?
Sol Habana
The Havana Sun

Margaret   in the midst of war
both yours & ours
How my country is trying to silence yours
How the silences here are many
& growing
        & the violence
not limited by nationality borders names

How people are more and more refusing
to be silenced
            in both our lands

Margaret   in the midst of war
from your letters of anger
                    & triumph
death struggle hope
you have sent me/shared with me
perhaps even as an afterthought
who knows?
        (& I will treasure it always)
a gift of light

Divisions

THE CASE OF JANE ALPERT

On November 14, 1974, Jane Alpert, who had fled underground
after having pled guilty to conspiracy in the bombing of government
property in the spring of 1970, surrendered to the United States District
Court of the Southern District of New York against the backdrop of
New York Post headlines in which she denounced her leftist past. This
event ended over two years as a fugitive and fueled a controversy within
the women's movement and the left that had started with a "letter from
the underground" which had been published in Off Our Backs a few
months before condemning the left and Sam Melville, her former lover,
who had been assassinated during the Attica uprising. The letter began:
"seeing this letter...here in print will shock you and that you will regard
much of its content as a breach of the tacit code of honor among political
fugitives..." and ended with the words, "And so, my sisters in
Weathermen, you fast and organize and demonstrate for Attica. Don't
send me clippings about it, don't tell me how much those deaths moved
you. I will mourn the loss of 42 male supremacists no longer." This letter
came attached to a document called "mother right: a new feminist
theory," Alpert's brand of feminism in which she argued that "female
biology is the basis of women's powers" and that the uprising of
women to come "...must be an affirmation of the power of female
consciousness, of the Mother."

Based on the "letter from the underground" which many felt had
divulged a lot of damaging information, word was privately circulating
around the movement that she had, as part of cutting a deal, been giving
detailed information to the FBI.

There is nothing as difficult to deal with as controversy within a
group of people you respect and consider your friends and peers,
particularly when you are all being beset by attacks from the outside.
Even though you can rationalize the necessity of such struggle, the
circumstances are trying and often can turn, at least temporarily,
extremely bitter. The Jane Alpert case was one of the worst in this
respect.

After Jane surfaced, a letter was circulated signed by many women
in the left condemning Jane for giving vital information to the FBI. At
that time, I felt there was no real proof either that she had done so or

what that information consisted of. What concerned me was not only the damage she might have already done but that future damage her case might cause. She was providing a rationale for giving information to the government at a time when the FBI was actively threatening women who refused to give information about the Lesbian and Feminist movements with being called up before Grand Juries and ultimately jailed. Several women, including Terry Turgeon, Ellen Grusse and Jill Raymond, were already serving jail terms simply for refusing to speak.

Jane Alpert was being presented as a feminist heroine and her conduct was being validated as the correct thing to do — it was all right to give information to the FBI as long as it was only about male chauvinist leftist men. It was in this spirit I co-authored the following statement, which appeared in the letters section of the April, 1975 issue of Off Our Backs:

THE CRISIS IN FEMINISM
To Women on the issue of Jane Alpert

It is the essence of oppression to set us against other oppressed peoples. To break our spirit. To set us against ourselves. To make us forget the real enemy. This is the strategy of the oppressor. It is a strategy we must recognize and struggle against wherever it shows itself, under whatever name it disguises itself. Particularly when it hides under the name of "feminism."

It is not war that destroys us, but betrayal. For betrayal destroys the heart and soul of our revolution. We are in crisis. Our honor, our integrity, our good faith are our primary weapons. We must not, can not, will not lose them. Our comrades underground are the seeds of our future. They are our pride. It is to these comrades in struggle we owe our deep and abiding loyalty. We can understand the pressures of the struggle and the traps it holds for us, but we reject anyone who betrays this loyalty as incapable of guiding or leading us.

Jane Alpert is not important, what is important is that women stop playing games, dangerous games, deadly games. There are two kinds of justice in this country. The system of justice for people like Jane Alpert, and the system of justice for people like Assata Shakur. Is this what we want the women's movement to represent? The kind of movement Jane Alpert represents. A movement based on class privilege, on white privilege. A racist movement completely cut off from our real needs.

It is time for us to take responsibility. To choose. We have declared our right to feel. Now we must declare and exercise our ability to think. To take responsibility for what we support and print. To recognize the implications and consequences of our ideas and actions.

Women can no longer afford to be silent on any issue that affects us in the core of our struggle. We are not isolated. We are engaged in a long struggle, a struggle with many battles and many battlefields. We are more than what we are as individuals. We are what we identify with. And our identification must be with all oppressed peoples. We do not "support" or "not support" the brothers of Attica. We *are* Attica. We are Attica or we are nothing. Not feminists, not women, not human beings. This is true feminism.

(signed)
Ti-Grace Atkinson
Joan Hamilton
Florynce Kennedy
Susan Sherman

The result was a furor greater than anything we could imagine. A statement signed by ninety well-known feminists was circulated supporting Jane and accusing us of promoting censorship.
I had been in long conversations at the time with Barbara Deming who had said she was unwilling to sign the statement supporting Jane and condemning us and was in the process of preparing her own statement. I remember the day I got it quite well. Because of a fire in the central office on Second Avenue over 150,000 phones in the area I live in were out of service. The only way you could call out was from

95

temporary phones that had been set up blocks away. The day I got Barbara's fourteen page letter — with a covering note to call her when I read it — it was pouring rain and the lines in front of the phones were interminable. When I finally reached her, I remember literally begging her not to print her letter because I felt it would only reopen the controversy and focus the issue again on Jane personally which would do a disservice both to the issues involved and, ironically enough, to June herself.

Barbara's letter addressed to me was printed — in both Off Our Backs and WIN magazine — and my reply, "Down the Rabbit Hole" appeared a month later in both publications. Barbara subsequently replied to my letter in "On the Subject of Trust...A Second Letter to Susan Sherman" which was published in WIN magazine in 1975 and finally an essay: "Seeing Us As We Are Not," which was rejected by every publication it was submitted to, in which she defends Jane Alpert and sees "Men on the right and on the left...acting together against us" and declares "Some women are breathing with them, too, without knowing what they are doing."

By this time I had taken myself out of the dialogue, having refused to reply to Barbara's second letter, feeling the whole issue had now become one of personalities rather than substance, and that our correspondence was in danger of turning into a polemic between Barbara Deming and myself completely obscuring what was really important. Later when the producers of a book of her essays asked permission to print my letter, I refused on the same grounds.

In 1981, Jane Alpert published Growing Up Underground in which she charged Robin Morgan, who had been one of her greatest supporters, with many of the same criticisms she had earlier reserved for Sam Melville and gave information that could be potentially damaging to other women who had supported her during her time underground.

"DOWN THE RABBIT HOLE"
(In Reply to Barbara Deming)

Reading your letter over, searching for a place to begin to answer it, I am reminded of nothing so much as the scene in *Through the Looking Glass* where Alice is confronted by the mad logic of Tweedledum and Tweedledee:

> "I know what you're thinking about," said Tweedledum, "but it isn't so, no-how."
> "Contrariwise," continued Tweedledee, "if it was so, it might be, and if it were so, it would be; but as it isn't, it ain't. That's logic."

The wonderful thing about words is that you can say anything with them. I can say, grass tree woman deer glass broke go run lightning fire, and it makes little outward sense. I can say: because all women can potentially bear children, they have something in common — Jane Alpert can potentially bear children — I can potentially bear children — therefore, Jane Alpert and I have something in common, and it seems not only to make perfect sense but to give some real information. (When, in fact, all I am saying is that Jane Alpert and I both have the potential to bear children.) I can then go even further and say: since all women have something in common, they are sisters — Jane Alpert is a woman — I am a woman — therefore, Jane Alpert is my sister, and seem to be making a perfectly logical and meaningful statement. However, since the first premise (since all women have something in common, they are sisters) is unproven and at best misleading, the conclusion has no more and probably a lot less to do with reality than grass tree woman deer. It is a fact of logic that if one accepts the premises, one is stuck with the conclusion — much like the fox who agreed to be judged by rabbits and then was surprised when they condemned her to death.

When Alice turns to greet Tweedledum and Tweedledee she doesn't know whose hand to shake first — she doesn't want to turn to one and hurt the other's feelings. "...so, as the best way out of the difficulty, she (takes) hold of both hands at once." And this is precisely what I feel you are doing in your "letter" — taking hold of "both hands at once." You've lived your life according to certain strong principles and judgments and now you're telling other women that's not the way to live. On the surface, your reasoning seems very considered and logical, and it *is* logical, but it built on basic premises and assumptions I find totally unacceptable.

For 2000 years at least, women have been told we didn't have the wherewithal to criticize, to make decisions — that we lacked the ability to make judgments, to choose. This was a role delegated to others — namely the males of the ruling class. In the context of the women's liberation movement and speaking as a feminist, you now tell us that "the old advice 'judge not' is now especially pertinent. A woman we may judge one day, met a few months later, can be quite different." In our original statement, "The Crisis in Feminism," we said:

> It is time for us to take responsibility. To choose. We have declared our right to feel. Now we must declare and exercise our ability to think. To take responsibility for what we support and print. To recognize the implications and consequences of our ideas and actions.

Five years ago, I struggled with some women on the *Rat* newspaper — ironically enough, about my Lilith poem — over the issues of publishing my poem without my name on it. I felt that women have been anonymous for hundreds of years, have been forced into anonymity, and as I was proud of and took full responsibility for the words, thoughts, feelings of my poem, I wanted my name on it. In fact, I would like to see people's names on everything they create. I would like to see their names on shoes, on clothes, on doorways, sidewalks, everywhere. I would like never to forget that so much of what makes my life possible is the creation of another human being.

And I feel exactly the same way about judgment, about choice, that I do about responsibility. Judgment — which means simply that you choose to do something because you feel it is the correct thing to do (rather than because you prefer to do it), that you choose to support or struggle against someone because you consider their actions correct or incorrect. And please don't tell me our lives are not made up of these choices, these judgments.

That you consider Madame Nu and Nguyen Thi Binh the same. That you didn't do everything in your power to stop one and support the other. The wonderful thing about words is that you can say anything with them.

Which leads directly to another of your premises — that we can't make judgments about women because women are constantly changing. Well, I certainly grant that things change and not always for the better, but what a blur, what a confusion to state that since women are in the process of change there's nothing we can say about an individual woman's actions. Confusion because in its overwhelming generality it leaves out the simple fact that individual situations differ and must be treated accordingly. Of course, you can't pressure people into understanding, everyone has their own rate of change. I am, personally, a very stubborn person. I resent certain kinds of pressure tremendously. I also don't feel any of us has the inside line on "truth." However, there are some basic things we can say.

Specifically, I really don't care how long it takes you to change your mind about your letter to me (although I certainly hope you do) but if you were to give evidence against me to the FBI that might result in a thirty year prison term, if you wrote a letter betraying every principle I believe in and set an example for others to do the same, giving women a rationale for betrayal — in other words, if you held a loaded gun to my head, I would certainly be worried less about your privilege to take your time changing your mind then I would be about how I was going to stop you. And if that gun was pointing to the head of someone I loved, someone I respected, whose struggle was my struggle, if that gun was a murderer's gun, I ask you, what would you do? Just how long would you wait?

"Judge not, lest ye be judged." That is the full quote from the Bible. I can only speak for myself, but I don't feel that being a woman gives me a blank check as far as my actions are concerned. I have made commitments to the people I love, to my work, to the struggle, and I feel very strongly that my life has meaning only in so far as I am loyal to, as I honor those commitments. I remember writing in 1966 in the first issue of IKON magazine:

The work of art is an embodiment of the process of choice. Each step a person makes constitutes a choice. An evaluation or judgment is the basis of choice. In order to make a judgment a person must be supplied with both the material to judge from and a method of judging. Movement is a dialogue, and the artist must engage in this dialogue, with themselves, with other artists, with their audience (that body which participates in their creation, without which their creation has no existence). There is no longer a place for the uninvolved.

And in 1971 in a poem called, "Ten Years After": "Life is a series of choices. By which we include or exclude all we ever hoped for or dreamed of. Love is a series of choices, by which we include or exclude the world."

What finally is struggle, but the attempt to change things, not randomly, but in a way that has meaning, that is not a betrayal, but a confirmation. I realize I have only dealt here with two or three of the basic points in your letter, premises on which you base your defense of Jane Alpert — whose actions it is obvious I consider absolutely indefensible, and which I feel were correctly and thoroughly analyzed in the statement by the women of the Weather Underground. (*Majority Report, April 19; Off Our Backs, May-June 1975*).

In order to make my own position absolutely clear, and because I express myself most precisely in my poetry, I would like very much to conclude with a poem which, in a very real way, grew out of this struggle:

AMERIKA
Fall, 1975

1.
How it comes
        in answer
    to a question
a way of being

                    included in
          of acting on

The fear of losing what we have
holds us immobile
The fear of losing what someday
                              we think
              we might get
keeps us from change

The real illusion
that we possess
                    anything
that anything possesses us
outside ourselves
                    our enemies
The gun held to our head

We are betrayed by objects
betray others   ourselves
through fear of loss

& lose everything

Amerika   you run through our veins
like oil   a surface slick
dissolving everything that breathes
that gives
          life
                    There is nothing I regret
but what has gone   undone
Amerika   this is your fever
your virus
          This fear

2.
For 35 years I have fought you
Inside/outside myself
your subtleties   your exaggerations

This lie that bore me
That I refuse to bear

What does it take to communicate
to make people understand
words seldom do it
                unless they cut
    beneath the surface
go down to the level where pain
begins   where all things give
birth
        Our fear is lost only
in that struggle
in the actions/words of those
who by refusing
                gain

What does it mean to communicate
to understand

3.
I break the surface
grasp for air
It is eight o'clock in the evening
a cold spring night
my anger buoys me past
the surface
            holds me
I gasp for life

Amerika   it is by choice
you are undone
                the courage to name things
To judge

By Terry Turgeon   Ellen Grusse and Jill Raymond
the women in New Haven and Kentucky
who refuse to speak
                By Assata Shakur

warrior
    and Sam Melville executed
in a prison yard at Attica
                By Lolita
Lebron Diana Oughton and Susan Saxe

Your enemies are endless   Amerika
Their very names a poem
               Be warned   Amerika
your agents spies and friends

By our life   we will finally
                  destroy you
Even as you try to level us
with your death

WOMAN AS CREATOR
AS POLITICAL BEING
TEACHER STUDENT AS WOMAN:
Sagaris & Process

This essay, completely revised for this edition, was first published in Charlotte Bunch and Sandra Pollack's anthology, Learning Our Way: Essays in Feminist Education. *It was originally commissioned by June Arnold for an anthology she was planning to publish on Sagaris which was cancelled when June fell ill. June's interest in the events at Sagaris was active and participatory and her death was a personal loss as well as a great loss to both the literary and feminist communities.*

In the summer of 1975, the feminist institute Sagaris held its first two sessions on the campus of Lyndon State College near Lyndonville, Vermont. Sagaris was intended to provide an alternative educational situation for women and develop the basis of a new feminist curriculum. The first session ended on the verge of chaos, and two and one-half weeks into the second session twenty-nine women (almost one-third of those present) including students, faculty members, children and assorted pets separated from the main group to form the August 7th Survival Community.

To understand what happened that summer at Sagaris is to understand how Sagaris mirrored the contradictions of our society as a whole, to talk specifically about the values of our society and how they consciously and unconsciously affect our actions and attitudes, individually and collectively, both when we accept or reject them.

The crisis that occurred at Sagaris resulted directly from the fact that the Sagaris collective, the eight women who then constituted the final decision-making body of Sagaris, saw Sagaris primarily as an institution, a thing, and not as a living network of intricate relationships, women engaged in thinking and sharing and learning in a specific place at a specific time.

The real irony is that because of the struggle which culminated in women formally separating from the original structure, Sagaris accomplished what it had set out to do — provide a place where feminist political theory could evolve, where the separation between thought and action could be resolved.

The Crisis at Sagaris

I still have a postcard on my desk of the Lyndon State College Campus. Shot from a distance, it presents the viewer with a bucolic scene of Vermont in the summer — the college nestled cozily among tall green trees against a background of softly rolling hills. In the foreground, three sheep are grazing in a large green meadow. Even the sky is a shade of greenish-blue. Amazingly enough, that was exactly the cliché that greeted us when we arrived on our first day — approximately one hundred and twenty students and a dozen assorted faculty members piling out of cars, vans, sometimes two, three, five at a time with luggage, books, back-packs. I had been hired to teach creative writing at Sagaris' second session and along with the required books and typewriter, I had even brought a small black and white TV, a possession which caused many sarcastic comments at the time, but was later to prove invaluable when we had to assume total responsibility for childcare in the alternative community.

It seemed almost too perfect. And perhaps a more experienced, less enthusiastic observer might have predicted from the beginning that isolating over one hundred women of all ages, interests, and levels of emotional stability along with some of the strongest, most diverse and opinionated voices in the feminist community on an isolated hill top for a period of five weeks would in itself be a dangerous thing to do. (The second session faculty included, among others, Ti-Grace Atkinson, Alix Kates Shulman, Jane Galvin-Lewis, Barbara Seaman and Marilyn Webb.)

The eight women who made up the Sagaris collective — among them writers, teachers and activists — claimed that Sagaris, as an institute of learning, had no partisan politics, that its purpose was to provide an educational forum for many radical feminist points of view, "to provide a framework, for women with prior involvement in women's issues, to study with some of the important feminist thinkers" (from a Sagaris brochure). The position

105

of the Sagaris collective would not be as a governing body *per se*, but as administrators. They would "facilitate", not direct.

In other words, within the general terminology "radical feminists," the stated position of the collective was to remain objective, detached.

But is it really possible for an administrative body to be totally objective? Decisions are always based on something. If the collective really had no specific commitment or set of values, it must, by default, make decisions on the basis of expediency — its own self-interest.

Sagaris was presented as a broadly based theoretical "think tank," and yet the choice that precipitated the second session split — *not just to accept, but to solicit* money from the Ms. Foundation — was, given the controversy surrounding Ms. at the time the funds were solicited, a highly charged, highly partisan political decision.

Sagaris had originally received $5,000 from the Ms. Foundation. Shortly after receiving that funding, charges were leveled concerning Gloria Steinem's involvement with the Independent Research Service, a group which was reputedly financed by the CIA. At the time the Sagaris Collective requested $10,000 more from the Ms. Foundation some two and a half months later, Steinem had still not answered those allegations. Consequently, some members of the Sagaris faculty, because of political stands they had taken and statements they had signed, could not possibly have accepted part of their salaries from the Ms. Foundation funding. To say nothing of the students and faculty who felt that, regardless of their own attitudes about Ms., compromising faculty in that way was totally unacceptable.

I will never forget the sinking feeling I experienced the day the announcement about funding was made by a member of the collective, casually layered between other miscellaneous bits of information. We were all gathered in the large school cafeteria — mealtimes often being the only time everyone could be found in one place. I remember vividly my stomach tightening into a small hard knot as everyone simultaneously stopped eating and the room became deadly quiet. I literally began to picture in my mind that pretty green Vermont postcard shredding slowly to pieces in front of my eyes.

The collective wanted it both ways: they wanted the Ms. Foundation funding and they wanted to avoid partisan politics. But you can't simultaneously act out both sides of a contradiction. The collective put themselves into a difficult situation and then, instead of analyzing what internal contradictions in the structure of Sagaris itself had brought them to this impasse, they threw the blame onto the dissenting students and faculty.

The Sagaris collective thus effectively put both students and faculty in a position of powerlessness within the institution — the traditional position of women in our society.

The Split

Once the collective solicited and accepted Ms. Foundation money, a split was inevitable. Women disagreeing with the decision of the collective were put in the further agonizing situation of having their loyalty to the women's movement called into question by their dissent — a classic, double-bind situation. If you said "yes," you compromised what you believed in and were committed to politically and were disloyal to your sisters. If you said "no," you were causing a "split" in the movement and were disloyal to your sisters.

It was no accident that the final crisis that split Sagaris was precipitated by an argument over funding, an argument the collective kept insisting was financial and not political. The first practical lesson you learn in any concrete situation, whether it is working with a local community group or living within the confines of a family, is that the person who holds the purse strings, who controls the money, holds political power — a lesson at which any woman should be an expert. Any power you gain is token if you have no power over the budget, over *where* you get money from and *who* you give it to. The collective as an *administrative* body controlling the budget was, in actuality, a *governing* body controlling Sagaris. The fight over Ms. Foundation money functioning as the catalyst that brought the internal contradictions which had plagued Sagaris since its inception to the surface: that

Sagaris, rather than being an alternative, was in reality a caricature of the traditional educational system.

Political power, at its best, moves people through a sharing of energy, making them strong enough to think and act on their own. At its worst, political power is a manifestation, pure and simple, of the ability to effect one's own self-interest by manipulating other people — either by making them feel powerless and dependent or by moving them from guilt and despair.

Everything was taken into consideration at Sagaris that summer except the possible needs of the women *as women*, collectively and as individuals, beyond their label as student, teacher, collective member. Sagaris presented its "alternative" course of instruction in a setting patterned after the traditional university system with no room for the complex human interaction which characterizes a true learning experience to develop. The "political theory" classes which were considered of primary importance were set off from the other courses. There was no attempt at coordinating different courses. Students, and for that matter faculty members, were given very little if any say over the organization of the school. The principle of fragmentation and the principle of hierarchy (the *division of* and the *division between*). The traditional system in action.

We fall back on archaic forms instinctively when we are insecure or in a hurry, when we become uncomfortable and face difficulties, when we are confronted with the anxiety of change, when we want to "make sure." Growth is possible only when we make a firm decision to close certain possibilities behind us, when we are not afraid to break down old institutions. When we are not afraid to leave.

The August 7th Survival Community

Given the increasing tension at Sagaris, the women who opposed Ms. Foundation funding decided to band together to discuss further action. The night of August 11, several women stayed up all night preparing a statement to be read the next day declaring that the question about funding was really a catalyst which brought to a climax contradictions that had been building since the first session: the high tuition costs, problems with child-care, inconsistencies in fiscal reports, the lack of real community input into either the structure of the school or its curriculum, the small number of working class women and minority women, the centralization of all real power in the collective.

On August 12, sixty-five women gathered into five clusters outside on the grass, a spot that would become a favorite place for meeting and discussion. (In fact, what most of the women would remember later was circle upon circle of women sitting on the grass discussing, debating issues of concern.) Each group that particular morning included both dissidents and women who had voted with the collective as well as at least one member of the collective.

It soon became obvious that nothing further could be achieved within the original Sagaris community, and finally twenty-nine women decided to separate completely from the Sagaris structure and set up an alternative community. A democratic structure was conceived which would involve classes, special events in the evening open to everyone, and one-time in-depth discussions. It was also decided that we would remain at Lyndon State College for room and board since those expenses were already paid and were nonrefundable. Some of the women also felt in order to make the most effective political statement it was necessary to remain at the Lyndonville campus in plain view of the women who elected to continue in the original Sagaris structure.

With the birth of The August 7th Survival Community, the crucial step had been taken from participation in an educational *institution* run by a collective of eight women to the formation of an alternative educational *community* run collectively by all the members of the community. And so began a struggle complicated by the pressures of a hostile environment, scant resources, the attitudes and prejudices of the community members themselves, and the overwhelming fact of there being so little time.

The August 7th Survival Community in many ways was a human miracle. A curriculum committee with a rotating member-ship was formed to make up a list of ideas about structure and scheduling, and each day time was set aside for community

109

meetings, collective decision-making, and criticism/self-criticism. In the space of two and one-half weeks, women who, with few exceptions, hadn't even known each other three weeks before, managed initially to put out a preliminary statement and later a full, detailed analysis of the Sagaris rebellion and Sagaris itself, print a newsletter, get a place in Lyndonville to hold meetings and classes, arrange collective childcare, and stay together through it all.

The division between faculty and students was nominally dissolved. All participants were invited to set up classes and events. Classes in Women's culture/poetry, the CIA, karate, theory construction, white feminists' view of racism, women's centers and journalism were initiated. Events that were set up included a concert, a tape on Emma Goldman, on women and prisons and a slide show on China.

But perhaps most important was the fact that basic questions, rather than being simply the content of lectures and intellectual abstractions, became a part of daily life.

In my creative writing workshop, we began a poetry mural project — each of us wrote and then printed, painted, drew poems on large sheets of butcher paper to be hung on community walls. As a result there was a change of emphasis from the workshop as an isolated creative experience to working in the context of a larger community. As a result, all our work, not just that specifically directed toward the mural project, became more animated and much more exciting. Women felt connected to one another organically in a way that had been totally lacking before the split, when our only real connection was that we happened to be in the same place at the same time studying the same subject.

Certainly holding true to the alternative community's goals of keeping "our structure flexible," "concentrating on process" and abiding by "majority decisions" was not without profound difficulties. As Sagaris caricatured the larger society, The August 7th Survival Community in many ways reflected the difficulties of the movement. While the collective for all intents and purposes ignored process, the August 7th Survival Community got so involved in the exploration of process there was often the danger of ignoring everything else — the syndrome of endless meetings, endless discussions and the resulting frustration and inertia.

Our society is exemplified by its expertise in the art of "double-think," the discrepancy between image and reality. In a commodity oriented society, everything is seen in terms of material advantage, whether something will depreciate (become less valuable) or appreciate (become more valuable) in *tangible* terms in the future. This is materialism at its crudest, permeating every aspect of our lives.

Until even relationships are seen as investments.

How these values actually work themselves out unconsciously in our attitudes toward ourselves and other people, particularly in a situation of struggle, is not always so clear. Consequently, we often exhibit the same prejudices, in a different framework, that we are working to destroy.

In a conventional educational community, status is determined by college degrees and expertise. This obscures the fact that while in our society *education* is mandatory, *learning* is considered valuable only in so far as it maintains and supports the establishment and is useful pragmatically "to get ahead." Apart from its utilitarian dollars-and-cents value, learning — knowledge itself — is considered a luxury and discouraged. *Learning* (an active verb) becomes synonymous in our minds with *being taught* (a passive verb). Education is then a concept so repulsive, so representative of oppressive authority, that we construct a block against acquiring the very skills we most need.

The need for proper credentials is no less a fact in most alternative structures. These credentials, if not merely identical to those of the establishment (or their exact opposite), are also often based on generalities and appearances. One way these attitudes expressed themselves in the alternative community was in the tension between former students and former faculty members — since that was one of the most obvious distinctions in an otherwise rather homogeneous group.

Defining problems in terms of a student/faculty hierarchy in the specific situation of Sagaris obscured two things. First, it blurred the differences between individual faculty members and, consequently, between the students. (Ironically, some of the students were faculty members in traditional universities, while many of the Sagaris faculty weren't.) But, most important, it made it harder to deal with the really essential questions of disparities between different levels and types of experience in the learning situation.

Two individuals relating to each other form a different dynamic from the two separately or in relation to anyone else, and each additional person changes the situation that much more. Group process sometimes results in relationships being cut off from their context, from the individuals interacting. A group is not an entity unto itself; it is the living relationships of the individuals who comprise it. To take all emotional and intellectual functions and put them into the primacy of the group is to change the group (society) from a collaborative of people into an artificial individual with a multiple personality of its own — an abstraction, and a schizophrenic one at that. The complex interaction of people becomes superseded by an anonymous group identity, in the process destroying the very thing which made the group possible to being with — the ability to stand up and fight oppression.

It is a primary responsibility of the individuals who comprise a collective not to allow it to take on the aspect of a dependent, oppressive, emotional relationship — jealous, demanding, possessive. To see that it doesn't become institutionalized.

The relation of the individual to the group, to other people, is the core question when one discusses politics, revolution, social change. Our community is the context in which we move, the background that brings our life into focus. Our choice of what community of people we move in is perhaps the most important choice of our life since it determines what we are, how we exist.

These were some of the important political questions the alternative community began to address — questions which, by their very nature, the original Sagaris could not speak to. But alternative community is really the wrong term. The name the community chose for itself was finally the most appropriate — the August 7th Survival Community.

112

Because the issue was more than finding an alternative structure, an alternative means of education; it was and *is*, in every sense, a question of survival.

What We Brought Away

The Sagaris split was not about two groups with differing politics engaged in a battle for control of an archaic structure. Even though, in retrospect, the worst failing of both the collective and the alternative community was inexperience, still in all the struggle of the August 7th Survival Community was against an oppressive act by a rigid system. It was a rebellion against constituted authority.

A new vision supersedes the old because it encompasses more, gives more, takes in new territory, leads us into new places. The violence associated with change comes from an establishment unable to tolerate what hits at its base, threatens its power, for whom a break-down of the established order is synonymous with chaos, the abyss, madness, death. But it is precisely change, growth, the breaking of oppressive structures and reordering them, that creativity, that politics is all about. Chaos doesn't result from change, which is a fact of life. Chaos results when the disintegration of a system is not accompanied by the birth of a new vision.

Chaos is not brought about by rebellion; it is brought about by the absence of political struggle.

No struggle is unimportant when people say *no* to a situation that oppresses them. The question is whether, once having faced the consequences of struggle, you continue to risk, continue to fight. *The real import of Sagaris is what we as women brought away with us — what it meant in our everyday lives.*

We carry our history, our values with us. Whether they are a burden or a source of energy depends on us.

Woman as creator as political being teacher student as woman. We struggle, we push against darkness, our own pain mute until the surface is reached. And then we begin. Always keeping in mind that, whatever new direction we take, we continue to carry ourselves.

August 1976; revised March 1990

Sexuality & Identity

LOVE POEM
FOR A CAPRICORN

With a hole in my stomach with four grey hairs with a
   callous on my toe with 32 years with 32 years
With a record player 53 albums desks and drawers and
   shelves of books rooms of thought I come to you
I come as water I come as rain as light falling great
   distances I come to you
I come to you in sleep as you walk as time
As tides form as illusion I come to you as night
   as sea
I come to you with death inside me with the pain of
   death inside me with what it means to leave
I come to you with nothing blind mute I come to you
As laughter I come to you as myself as hair hands eyes
   sex I come to you
In madness in love I come to you in minutes hours seconds
   in walking running swimming crawling flying
With a dirty apartment I come to you with an empty
   refrigerator with a house full of cats
I come to you as water comes to earth as the sea reaches
   toward the sand
As lover as friend I come to you as necessity as need

A POEM

for you alone
built word upon word
like years
like time people share
together
deepening
growing into meaning
word
upon word
meaning
upon meaning
for you alone a poem

I know your need for form
for things to be
concrete
the way grass moves & light
the borders
of your shoes
the mountains
of your home
all these things
a kind of boundary
a definition
a name

if I could offer you the salt taste
of the sea
if I could turn your home
into a glance
a gesture
of the eyes
if I could look at you as home
speak to you as sea

there is nothing on this earth
that does not change

that does not deepen or drift
away

there is nothing on this earth
more concrete
            than this feeling
        I have
                now
for you

nothing
is more
        real

AS WHEN THINGS FIT

The sun has finally come out
I waited all morning
Nothing moved
Rummaging through my wallet
I found a piece of mint
A luxury
      those days
          you said
As when things fit together
As we never fail   if possible
to shut each other out
so slow to understand
what almost every other creature knows
                      instinctively

What it means
to re-discover words
fill them with meaning
strip their labels
         their common use
Today   sifting through my poems
filtering years
seeing those words fit together
The sum of all moments
until now
     I am tired
of seeing people I love
           places
move by
I know the truth of my poems
have lived their blood
In all these years I have discarded
nothing
     They are not memory

are pieces of my own body
These words

Is it so strange then   knowing this
that I am reluctant to give up
To separate myself
To tolerate another
                     separation
Knowing quite simply
how rare it is   how seldom it happens
That things fit

DAY DREAM

This air we live in each day
is so thin
           it would crack
if we looked too hard at it
I want you to come home with me
I want to soak my eyes
in you   Slide my forehead
against your touch
hear your voice   soft
the way voices are
               in that place
I would not reach forward
violently   instead
would hold back ever so
slightly
        & then
I would be there for you
Always there for you
As you lifted yourself
                  soft
against our need

But I too make choices
& obviously   I am not one
of yours
Except perhaps in fantasy
                    that safe place
dry as an old sandwich
mildewed & rare

HORIZON

There's a story about musicians
that is seldom told
How sometimes
         in later life
they begin to hear one note
constantly
         singing
through their ears
A physical illness with a
fancy name
it drives them mad

How then can I blame you
for choosing another route
Having heard it
         That dreadful note
faint on the horizon
Its deadly background
The risk

A FARE/WELL PRESENT

Well   good-bye
and all that means
if in fact it means
anything
            words sometimes
taking the place
of meaning
                  like last night
twisted in my own
syllables   trying
to explain

Or that summer
seven years old
first time away from home
A feeling of the heart
but literally that
                  The camp director
calling it "homesick"
or "missing"
Not only that something
was missing
            that I was missing
someplace or someone
but that somehow
I was also missing
from something   somewhere
I wanted to be

A seven-year-old pride
denied it   denies it still
but now with how much more vehemence
command of language
skill with words
                  no longer only
(shoulders out   chest squared)
"homesick   not *me*"

but paragraphs of explanation
reams of words
              to say only
somewhere something
has been left out
is out of place

And so   as a farewell present
I give you this poem
This feeling of the heart
That when I think of you
leaving
         And when I think of you here
and can't be with you
Even when we are together
when I feel you growing distant
I experience that
            "missing"
that something
left out
as if I am discovering the word again
for the first time
What it really means

As with all things that move us
deeply
       the feeling comes
                first
the experience
As we perceive the meaning
The word
       follows later
"missing"

that space which is not empty
but fills all space

DURATION

Many nights I waited   Many years   The words
slow in coming   Often I called   There was seldom
an answer   The magic beneath my feet   At my
fingers   Often I dreamed   To find truth different
from the dream

The earth is a strange lover   Beauthful in its face
Who looks to the earth for love
Looks into death

Many nights I waited   Many years   Until the words came
Their form like the earth   Beautiful in their face
To understand is to know in just what way I
walked   The dream that drove me forward
That rests with me still

My friend   As I reach to touch you   So still you are
So near   There is a truth a mirror cannot tell
To understand the dream   To hold it close
As hands   As eyes

When it is so cold the fingers grow chill
When there is no speech because the stillness
must not be broken   When even poems must cease

If I could give you anything   I would give you
this dream   In its contradiction   In its truth
How in action it changes   What in action
it means   How the earth opens its body   Almost
as an act of grace

WOMEN, IDENTITY, SEXUALITY:
A Re-examination

Edited from a talk presented at the Franco-American Feminists' Conference at Paris, France, Summer 1982 sponsored by Columbia University of New York.

A human being does not live in isolation. Our community is the context in which we move, the background that brings our lives into focus. Conversely, our community is defined by who we are, what we bring to it. An examination of this interrelationship of the individual to the group, to other people, to history is basic to any discussion of "identity." What people we choose to surround ourselves with is one of the most important choices we make. And no less important is whether that choice is ours to make.

It is a truism that one way of keeping an oppressed group in their place is to deny them their identity by subsuming them as anonymous beings, beings without individuality, into the hierarchy of the oppressor. Women are not, in fact, in patriarchal society and ideology, even the so-called "existential other." We are not even one side of the duality male/female. In reality, the position of "other" is reserved for the male — the "feminine" is a part of the male — the sensitive artist, the "obedient" priest (the "bride" of Christ"), Jung's "Anima." Even the slave in Hegel's famous exposition of the master/slave relationship is a man. Woman as a *living* being exists on another, a lower level. She is elevated to an equal position as "other" only in man's fantasy life, only as a symbolic psychological representation of some part of *himself* — Goethe's Beatrice, Conrad's unnamed forest woman in *Heart of Darkness* contrasted to the European woman he must protect. The examples are legion. The *living, breathing* she has no identity and so, in order *even to assume the position of adversary*, an identity must first begin to be forged. An identity must be created alongside any successful political struggle before we can be truly liberated from oppressive definitions and stereotypes, group anonymity, the "biological imperative" and perhaps, most important, the acceptance of violence as an integral part of our lives.

Sexuality & Identity

Our identity as women has been most often defined and analyzed traditionally under the category "sexuality" because women's source of power and use has been traditionally conceived of by patriarchal society as based in our sexual organs either as a source of male pleasure or the place of the conception of children. The oppression of women as a class is known as "sexism." Consequently women have been defined traditionally solely by their relationships with their sexual partners — both within and outside the family unit. Women operate within these limited relationships as *sexual beings,* whether as mother, wife, mistress, lover. While the male, by virtue of his privileged status, is an independent being, a being with self-identity, the female is identified as a dependent being and her dependency is always relative to a masculine/dominant figure and is always sex-related, including the fruits of sexuality — motherhood and children.

The point here is not that women have been traditionally defined primarily as sexual beings by men — that is hardly news — but that after all these years, after all these books, articles, essays, discussions, that sexuality continues to be overwhelmingly the perspective by which women are seen both by men *and by other women.* This includes all categories of sex-dependent relationships including the matriarchy, lesbianism as sexual choice, heterosexual feminism that sees feminist struggle literally as the battle of the sexes, certain kinds of women's spirituality that ritualize women's sexuality, as well as the latest phase of punk S&M. A man is spoken of as worker, artist, intellectual, scientist, soldier, revolutionary and is rarely seen as father, husband or even as lover except in extravagant proportions — lover with a capital L. Women's rights and concerns are often grouped under titles like "reproductive rights," and are restricted to issues like abortion, birth control, sexual choice.

Political issues like "reproductive rights," and economically related issues like childcare are *absolutely essential* in determining our ability to choose and act free of outside coercion. And certainly now more than ever when those rights are being rapidly eroded. However, in addressing these questions are we addressing a necessary problem, vital to our self-*interest*, or are we, in reality, using these problem areas to define our self-*identity* — thereby unconsciously submitting to the standard subservient biological role women are placed in daily by a patriarchal culture which sees men as human beings, varied and individual, and women as a homogeneous grouping — identical, one-dimensional, sub-human.

The first questions when addressing the issue of "women and identity" then must be: Does using the term "sexuality" to epitomize women's situation mystify rather than clarify the underlying attitudes and assumptions responsible for women's subjugation, including her sexual subjugation? Is it possible that as long as "woman" is defined as a sexual term, as child-bearer, as sexual appendage (even "valued sexual relationship"), sexuality will, rather than being seen as one aspect of our life, continue to be our all-defining context?

Most importantly, the answer to these questions can clarify or obscure the crucial question of how the issues of racism and economic class specifically affect women's relationships to — *images of* — each other and the outside world.

Self & Social Identity

If it is the case that our perception of the world is to a large extent based on our needs, it is also true that our needs are determined both by who we define ourselves to be and others' definitions of us — by our *self*-identity and our *social* identity. While it is true the two overlap, that the political and personal are mutually interdependent and inseparable, it is equally true that the two terms — "personal" and "political" — *are not identical*, are not reducible one to the other, and that perhaps this is where much of the confusion begins. Without political activism, a sense of being part of a larger struggle, questions of self-identity become isolated and fanciful; without a sense of personal identity, political activity is empty and without focus.

The contradictions between the personal and political become apparent in situations of crisis, when the two clash. The controversies revolving around issues like the Left and feminism, lesbian and heterosexual identity, separatism, racism, classism, ageism are not superficial, they are based on real social situations as well as theoretical differences and social conditioning. It is possible however that many of the controversies surrounding these issues are further complicated by a reductionism which is a by-product of patriarchal methodology, by not considering basic assumptions that underlie traditional patriarchal philosophy and which, consequently, operate subconsciously. As a result of which we tend to turn to the past for relief — either to a mythic antiquity, to the way things were before feminism went astray (e.g. before lesbianism became a focal issue), to 19th century based psychology, or at its extreme, to the time before feminism entered the picture altogether and got the "real issues" all confused.

Self-identity for the patriarchy is always bought at the expense of "the other."[1] Not only is duality defined as opposition, but conflict is proscribed as a basic category of human existence. For classical patriarchal thinkers motion, change, the physical world, material existence itself is caused by a state of imbalance. The classical ideal of the universal rests on a concept of timelessness predicated on perfect balance, perfect measure, perfect form — ideals that do not exist in the mundane world, a physical world denied any value except as a testing ground for the intellect, or, in the more liberal patriarchal philosophers, the place where the laws of the intellect are, by necessity disclosed. This is even more true of modern structuralist or psychologically oriented philosophies which eliminate the idea of balance in favor of a syntactically organized theory of human disorientation and conflict.

Violence against Women

Not only are we dealing here with duality, but with the concept that our life is *by necessity* one of violence and conflict. Consequently, one side of the duality must always be subjugated by and/or subsumed under the other. Rather than using the

130

relative ethical construct "good/bad" to judge actions within a class, classes and qualities *in their entirety* are divided into the now primal categories "good" and "evil." (e.g. Black is evil, white is good; feminine is bad, masculine is good; passion is evil, thought is good; night is evil, day is good etc.) According to these men, whether it is internal or external, it is conflict that sets us in motion. It is war that purifies us. Whether we dominate other people or nature, it is "strength," forcefulness, that "makes a man a man." These ideas on violence are basic assumptions about the nature of existence that run through virtually all of the history of ancient and modern male thought — even in those men who restore the physical to a primary position.

By the middle of the 19th century, Hegel, certainly one of the most important influences on modern social history, brought this ideology to a new level by describing the benefits that accrue to being placed in the inferior position in his now famous presentation of the "master-slave" relationship:

> ...the slave...in the service of the master, works off his individualist self-will, overcomes the inner immediacy of appetite, and in this divestment of self and in 'fear of his lord' makes the 'beginning of wisdom' — the passage to universal self-consciousness.... *Slavery and tyranny are, therefore, in the history of nations a necessary stage and hence* relatively *justified*...[2] (Italics mine).

Hegel goes on to state that, in any case, unless a man is willing to risk his own life *and others* for freedom, he deserves to be a slave.

This blatant ideology of domination is presently exemplified by movements which define pain as a necessary part of life and dominance as an innate quality of human existence. Ironically, disguised as rebellion, punk and S&M, for example, ritualize the very heart of a patriarchal justification of brutality towards women derived from the belief that the desires of the physical world, the world of the senses — which are the main barrier to enlightenment and immortality — must be forcibly disciplined through mortification of the flesh.

And who is the living symbol of this deceptive world of the senses? Who seduces man to his doom? Woman. This is, in fact, the basic assumption behind the male justification of why women have to be kept in their place — forcibly, if necessary.

Violence against women — an everyday condition of our lives. As one woman so aptly put it, "Think of the relief you feel, any woman feels, when you realize the shape at the far end of the deserted street is a woman, not a man." It confronts us physically; it confronts us psychologically. It is part of every image on every level that we incorporate into our own self-image. The core issue isn't sex. Images of violence against women are destructive whether they occur on 42nd Street in a porno house, in a fashion magazine, on a record cover, in a touted work of "great" literature, or in the Bible. And, once again, we must examine how we are conditioned into accepting violence as an integral part of our own identity.

If you accept the transferal of the medieval devil from the netherworld to the recesses of our psyche and make it the source of our most basic (read:sexual) energy — as Freud does with his amoral, aggressive, selfish life *force* the Id[3] — images of violence play a necessary role in keeping human beings under control, allowing them to let off steam in fantasy rather than reality. If, on the other hand, you believe that images have an educational effect, that they play a vital role in shaping our self-image, our self-identity and keeping us in line, then you believe images of violence are a cause of violent activity rather than a safety-valve, you implicitly assert that violence is not a "given" of human existence.

Nationalism: Cultural & Revolutionary

Our self-image, our identity, determines both the choices we make and whether we act on these choices — whether we think we are capable of acting in our own or others' behalf. That is why *all political struggles have first been struggles bound up with identity and have had strong nationalistic elements.* One of the most important documents to cover the concept of women's identity in this way is the essay "The Woman-Identified Woman." Written by Radicalesbians and published in 1970, it still stands as one of the most important theoretical documents on feminist identity.

Defining lesbianism as first and foremost a question of identity in which a woman in a male-dominated society rebels against the subservient role foisted on her — the *female role* — it also separates women from the heterosexual privilege that comes with the acceptance of that role. "Woman-Identified Woman"[4] recognizes the sexual act *as an act of love* — determining who we value, spend time with, give our loyalty to. Lesbianism is seen as a way to true autonomy, to individuation — a necessary step in any acculturation process.

> Until women see in each other the possibility of primal commitment which includes sexual love, they will be denying themselves the love and value they readily accord to men, thus affirming their second-class status.

And furthermore,

> As long as male acceptability is primary — both to individual women, to the movement as a whole — the term lesbian will be used effectively against women.[5]

"Woman-Identified Woman" was an important document because it spoke of the positive potential of women asserting themselves as independent individuals, no longer needing men to validate their identity. It spoke of "women-loving women." It empowered women, in the full knowledge that a woman who feels powerless is a woman unable to choose or act.

With this essay and the lesbian movement, a burst of new energy propelled the feminist movement forward. But could the other parts of the feminist movement discuss these new ideas, grow with them, change them if necessary to fit their own needs, taking part in the process of refining and shaping these ideas into a more mature form. Most could not. "Woman-Identified Woman" as a theoretical document was limited. Any document is. It was only a beginning. It did not adequately cover questions of economics and racism. The idea of cultural feminism was vague and led to misunderstandings still with us today — due to its association (intentional or not) with cultural nationalism, a term which referred to separatist struggle not necessarily connected to any other type of radical change. Cultural nationalism was juxtaposed in turn to "revolutionary nationalism" — nationalism dedicated to coalition with others if necessary in the fight for radical social change.

It was also argued that "Woman-Identified Woman" implied that lesbianism *per se* was revolutionary even though the essay stated quite clearly that:

> ..irrespective of where our love and sexual energies flow, if we are male-identified in our heads, we cannot realize our autonomy as human beings.[6]

Even though "Woman-Identified Woman" stated that to see lesbianism as purely sexual was divisive and sexist, it did not address clearly enough the position of feminists who chose to continue the struggle as heterosexuals. And, unfortunately, attacks contained in articles like "The Pseudo-Left/Lesbian Alliance"[7] — and the ensuing conflict — made a even greater schism in the movement.

The women's movement in the 70s was not diverted by the lesbian movement — the lesbian movement was one of the main sources, if not the main source, of energy that kept the women's movement alive. If anything, the feminist movement suffered a lull in the late 70s because of several related factors — first, the inability of the original groups to adjust to changing circumstances; second, by the temporary successes in struggles for abortion and women's rights; and, finally, by a self-destructive isolationism by heterosexual and lesbian women alike, who drew into their own respective communities and turned away from fighting for fundamental change and toward fighting either for equal rights within the prevailing system or for separating off within it — along with the attendant lack of identification and coalition with other political struggles.

This statement is not an attack on the autonomous women's movement or all-women organizations which were and are *absolutely necessary*. Also, this entrenchment was not peculiar to the women's movement which, in those years, was one of the most active forces for social change. It would be a tremendous mistake to ignore the intense energy expended and the great achievements made during this period.

Identity & Struggle

In the United States today we are confronted negatively by the re-activation under Reagan of overt and concentrated activity that threatens every one of the gains we have made and positively by the creative energy coming from an emerging indigenous Third World women's movement. The perspective of Third World women in the United States is far from homogeneous, but generally, in terms of issues like their relationship to their own national culture, their situation is different in many respects from that of white feminists. Rigid feminist separatism under these circumstances can't speak coherently to the issues these women raise — even though many of them are also lesbians. Third World women have been in the movement, have been in the leadership of the movement, from its beginnings. What is new now is that *communities* of Third World women are asserting their feminist identity and they, *as women,* have gathered strength and become the main energy force within the women's community as a whole. There are a number of excellent resource books that have come out over the last few years that speak eloquently and with great power to these issues.[8] *What happens now to the American women's movement may well rest on how well this new transition will be made. Whether white lesbian women will make the same mistakes heterosexual women did in the past.*

These are all issues that become increasingly important to clarify in order to deal with another social transition, the far-reaching implications of computer technology which affects every aspect of our lives — from the work-place to the school to the home. It is unfortunately more and more the standard of our times to see things, helped by this technology, in a way that distorts and mystifies them — in statistical patterns rather than individual events and historical process, through re-presentation rather than direct experience.[9]

As we drift further and further, carried by the current of contemporary events, it becomes increasingly necessary to set our own course, to refuse to be intimidated — at the same time remaining flexible enough to change as conditions change.

This seems obvious, but the obvious is often the hardest thing to act on and the most difficult to see. As human beings living in an ever-shrinking world, we exist in a situation of mutual dependency. We carry that set of relationships which is our society with us. Unless we understand the forces that move us, we perpetuate oppression. We become involved in actions that are self-defeating. We mimic the oppressor.

With years of experience behind us, it is time now to re-evaluate the relationship of identity and struggle — remembering that a change in labels, in outward form, is meaningless unless it grows from a change in attitude and is accompanied by action. Not just a shifting of priorities, but a radical alteration in our way of existing in the world.

FOOTNOTES

1. Specific examples are legion. Modern examples include Hegel, *The Philosophy of Mind*; Sartre, *Being and Nothingness*; Jung on individuation; even Merleau-Ponty, *Phenomenology of Perception*.
2. Hegel, *Philosophy of Mind*. Oxford at the Clarendon Press: London. p. 175.
3. For clarification of this point of view: Sigmund Freud *Civilization and its Discontents*, The Hogarth Press and the Institute of Psycho-Analysis: London.
4. Karla Jay & Allen Young (eds.), *Out of the Closets: Voices of Gay Liberation*. Douglas/Links: New York. p. 174.
5. *Ibid.*
6. *Ibid.*, p. 175.

7. Redstockings, *Feminist Revolution*. Redstockings, Inc.: New Paltz, N.Y. "The Pseudo-Left/Lesbian Alliance," pp. 189-194.

8. Gloria T. Hull, Patricia Bell Scott, and Barbara Smith (eds.), *All the Women are White, All the Blacks are Men, But Some of Us Are Brave: Black Women's Studies*. The Feminist Press: Old Westbury, N.Y., 1982.

   Cherrie Moraga, Gloria Anzaldua (eds.), *This Bridge Called My Back: Writings of Radical Women of Color*. Kitchen Table: Women of Color Press: Lathem, New York, 1984.

   J. R. Roberts, *Black Lesbians: An Annotated Bibliography*. The Naiad Press. 1981.

   Erlene Stetson (ed.), *Black Sister: Poetry by Black American Women*, 1746-1980. Indiana University Press: Bloomington, Indiana. 1981.

   Beth Brant (Degonwadonti) (ed.), *A Gathering of Spirit: North American Indian Women*. A collection by Firebrand: Ithaca, New York, 1989.

9. An interesting presentation of the philosophical implications of technology is presented in Martin Heidegger's *Questions Concerning Technology and Other Essays*, particularly in the essay, "The Age of the World Picture," p. 115. Harper Colophon Books.

AREAS OF SILENCE

1.
To startle the past into order. To break the miles.

If it is possible to talk about people, it is possible to talk about love. If it is possible to talk about the city, warm, under the rain, it is possible to talk about love.

Words are no more than the objects they represent. To touch them the way one touches plaster, the window glass, the stickiness of a moist humid afternoon. Knowing it is not that anything is forbidden, but that the past does not easily shape itself into form.

The sound of your voice is the sound of my fingers trying to construct images. As if each word must be physically molded, formed, shaped into existence. The way letters curve. And then forgotten. Formed. And then forgotten.

To recognize everything must be written. That even the introduction is essential.

That even without us, the sidewalk defines the same pattern.

2.
The street is bare in the rain. Quiet. Music from the apartment house filters unevenly through the mist. Everything seems to be just behind me as I walk. The music. The sound of people talking, arguing, singing. The present becomes as distant as the faintness of concrete walls and odors mingle with the salt of your own flesh.

It is difficult to retain the freshness of experience if one is not willing to face the strangeness and horror of it. To believe it as it is. To accept, not the past, but the footsteps that create it.

A drunk slips to the sidewalk. He lies there, the rain bouncing against his arm. I stand for a moment, looking at him.

The sidewalks dissolve. Not a path stretching endlessly to no certain point, but no path at all. To try only to avoid facility, to relate without judgment. No. To allow the possibility of anything. Even of facility. Even of judgment. To allow each unit of experience to build its own set of existences. To start from any point in any universe. To start with a drunk stretched across the rain.

3.

Years. To be able to see what it was that linked us, binding us together as irrevocably as that boat carried me from the city, from the details of your face, your body, your words.

I trace my memories with your form and because you are no longer a part of my body, no longer anything except the part of me which can reach through distance, I can define the present. Knowing memory binds one to the present.

You made the mistake of thinking by arousing feeling in me, my feeling would be directed toward you. As if you could control my past, my blood, my memories. As if these things were yours to control.

The boat moves forward, unaware of the distances it forces to the pattern of its motion.

If you could believe the roles could have been enacted by anyone. It was inevitable that the events should have somehow been created.

I rub my finger across the rain, touch my hair, wishing it were yours. Trying to center you in the city, catch you in the square of its sidewalks. Knowing even then it would take more distance than water.

It is not that the ocean acts as a boundary or even a space, but that the smallest parts of it somehow separate us from ourselves. As if the water could recognize us and in that recognition we could lose the parts of ourselves described as unique.

Turning, I watch the land grow smaller, moving backward, shrinking into itself. I watch the foam break, white, against the edge of the boat. The smell of the water, the wind, tight against the corners of my face.

We are one person now. One action. One voice.

Where is the measure that can separate us?

4.

How strange — hearing from you. After so long. I think of myself, of how much I must have changed. Of how inaccurate my picture of you, as you exist now, must be. You write me the details of your life. They mean nothing to me. The people you mention I do not know. The people I know do not exist for you. I wonder sometimes what it was I loved — how many people went into the conception I loved as you. I suppose that more than anything else I wanted something to give meaning to my life. I wanted that one thing to be a single person. And unable to find what I wanted, I created it.

5.

In early evening when color seems to stand apart from the objects which hold it, I sometimes walk along the edge of the pavement, and staring into the faces of people who pass me, see your face.

Remembering how we walked through empty mornings. The only interruption the sound of an occasional bus. The crisp silence breaking the sidewalks into a path for our feet only.

It is only in those moments I remember it was through you I discovered my own hands, my own eyes, my own flesh.

We move toward each other, merge, move away, move toward another shape — different only because of the path of our motion.

If I never saw you as you see yourself. If I must create you now, years later, say if you can I cannot understand the world you felt once, feel now.

If somewhere, in some universe, you still exist.

6.

To want something beautiful so much you are willing to give up everything to create it. And then to find it is something you cannot touch.

To want to feel your own body so much, you realize it is made up of more than the number of bodies that have known it, that it has known.

Until whatever it is that calls itself by our name goes its own way, scarcely caring whether we follow or not.

The city leans toward me. Watching the people. Watching the rain. It breaks. Folds. I see you in front of me, your hands moving in circles, separating the space around you. The miles I walk on the moist pavement. As if by walking, I could become part of your hands, your space.

I turn. Leave the drunk behind me, lying, face down, on the sidewalk. The rain has stopped and people crowd into the street. I move against the dampness of my clothes, voices surrounding me like the hollow sound of the rain.

7.

So much length. And the hunger. The afternoon, hot, crawls through the room. So many faces. And the hunger. A record spins and spins and spins and somewhere a child lies against a distance of broken afternoons.

I think sometimes there must be more than this: the words, the heat, the distance of memories. But then in action, so strange, and always the hunger and always the dreams.

Ahead the walls expand. My foot reaches to their distance. But always they move. Further. Further. My mind cannot grasp their immeasurable distance.

If it were possible to break your motion with my hands, I would do it. I talk to you, knowing you are not listening to me. Even as I talk, my words become yours, my face becomes yours. When I finish, I will no longer exist except as part of you. Do you think it is easy for me? Do you think my hands are the whole of it, that the way they move defines my motion? If I could, I would kill you as you stand there destroying me with my words. If I could, I would kill you. If only to convince you of my existence apart from you.

141

The walls expand I can no longer hold their space.

8.

Treading the night between my heels. Each step, a step of which I am unaware. Later, I mark the length of each footprint, of each block. Of each city. But now, as I walk, I walk without logic. Without instinct.

A dog lies asleep in the dirt. His muzzle buried deep in the rich, brown dust. He scarcely breathes. Thin — he seems to have grown there, to have sprung up suddenly and quietly, like some strange plant.

My steps sound too lonely in the street. My name forcing me into a unity which mocks me. With names — a story of lines, of spaces, of intervals. The miles I walk. The fragments I hide.

But sometimes, you see, I don't care. Riding a bus. watching people move around me. Fat, with years of starch, with years of work. Poor, with years of feeding children into a city alien to even the inflection of their speech. Sometimes I share their fat, their dislocation. Sometimes I laugh through their eyes, bend with their muscles. Free of the past and the names that define me.

To travel so fast there can be nothing but this. To speed past the arguments, the reasons, the attempts at unity. The attempt to find a point at which each point is definable.

My steps sound too lonely. My footprints forcing me into a space, a way of speech. Knowing the arguments, the reasons, the compensations, the rewards, the desire. Knowing the desire.

But sometimes I touch my own flesh. And only that it is my flesh. And only that it is soft to my touch.

Sometimes, you see, I just don't care.

9.

Words — no more than the outer edge of silence. What have we left to say, you and I. The dozens of us crowded into a single space, a parallel moment. The words. Written. Spoken. The time etched between each syllable.

That is part of it. But only a part.

The cold creeps around the edges of my shoulder. Listening. Thinking. At this moment only. And then.

And then?

It is not of death I am afraid, but the moment before death. It is not action that makes me afraid, but consciousness.

What have we to say to each other, more than this?

I hold your hand, feel your pulse against my arm. Caught in a moment of desire, I fall. Backward. Heavy. Thinking that finally here. Here.

There is no escape. There is no turning back.

To move is to be touched. To be flung, lucid, against the inner layers of the rain.

To know is to touch. To be killed by the sun.

New York, 1963

The Counterfeit Revolution:
McLuhan, Derrida, Lacan

THE TYRANNY OF FORM

In the 1960's, Marshall McLuhan, prophet of the new age and one of the first to realize the importance of the new electronic technology, wrote a counter-culture best seller, *Understanding Media*. In it, he predicted electronic technology would truly liberate an alienated and fragmented humanity. The fabled "Age of Aquarius" was finally dawning. Through advanced communication techniques, the world community, the "global village," was a real possibility. We could now, at long last, move from being overly dependent on our visual sense, a consequence of adopting reading as our chief method of learning, and rediscover the interdependency of all our senses, a true unity of perception, as a result of the increased use of audio-visual and mixed media. Moreover, for McLuhan, watching TV was biologically liberating because we are called on to creatively and actively construct the image which is the TV picture from a spectrum of dots, as opposed to the physical passivity of reading a book with its set type.

Quite simply, for McLuhan and his followers, the new media would change our whole way of being in the world. The age old duality between mind and body, thought and sensation, would finally be laid to rest. And all this would eventually happen *because of the nature of the media itself*. The movement from the mechanistic, materialistic, deterministic model which emerged from the Industrial Revolution and the paradigm of the machine to the new non-linear, non-sequential model of electronic media would happen *regardless of the specific content* of the media. Because the real content of the media is its form. It is the media itself and not its subject matter that "informs" (in-*forms*) the viewer. Hence the meaning of the famous rallying cry, "The medium *is* the message."

The Emperor's Old Clothes

It is only a small step from McLuhan's speculations to the more sophisticated proponents of modern "information theory" with their argument that information theory and electronic technology coupled with new discoveries in biology provide us *ex post facto* with a way out of the dilemma of the one-dimensional approach to the world generated by the Industrial Revolution. Old nineteenth century words like "forces," "drives," "energy" are already being replaced by the new jargon: "probability," "redundancy," "complexity," "entropy." The new theories are proclaimed life-based and complex as opposed to simple and mechanistic. Information theory is biological rather than mechanical. It is grounded in the "logic of life" rather than on the algebra of the machine. Organic math replaces the conventional equation.

It is important to note the new constellation of disciplines that is arising as a result of the emphasis on information theory and computer technology. As the old mechanism was grounded in physics, (particularly Newtonian physics,) information theory, its replacement, is grounded in biology, as evidenced in DNA coding; in behavioral psychology, with the emphasis on learning theory; in those parts of philosophy relating to language, specifically that branch of semantics devoted to the study of structures and logic. There is a strong emphasis on statistics and probability theory; the procedural language is mathematical computation. And, of course, the catalyst and *raison d'etre* of this new alliance is computer programming.

Information theory owes a large debt to the theories of Claude Shannon who formalized ideas of communication based on his work with radio and the telephone — what noise is, how much "redundancy" is necessary to ensure the recovery of information, how entropy is an important component of communication. Some of these concepts were rendered mathematically by Shannon. The tie-in with people comes from the fact that the radio, telephone, television, computers, human beings (not only consciously, but *in their very genetic make-up*) are all information processors and symbol manipulators — transmitting information through coding, actively "informing" their environment, not only changing or effecting, but, in a very real sense, creating their world.

Information is not viewed here as a passive *thing*, it is an active *process*. In fact, what we are seeing is the whole definition of communication and information as we think of it undergoing a subtle transformation. The two are actually merging into one concept in which what we think of as information (consisting of data that we, as human beings, interpret and then choose whether to use) and communication (which is the process by which data is transmitted) becoming first a unified process — literally "informing" us — and then an abstract process — one that takes place in the world of mathematical probability and statistics rather than mundane activity. *Real creative activity, if you follow this argument to its logical conclusion, is thereby moved out of the realm of human interpretation and choice altogether. What creates, orders, chooses the world, what "in-forms" it, is the medium or, in the new lingo, the "code" itself.* Everything becomes subsumed under the code, which is now a biological process: the sender, the receiver, the message, the means and method of sending, the means and method of interpretation. The computer program disassociates itself from the programmer and user and goes its own way.

It is McLuhan on a new and, before computer technology, hitherto unimaginable level.

Formalism in its shiny old clothes.

Scientific "Objectivity" and Human Understanding

Objectivity in our modern 20th century American high tech world means much the same thing as it has for Western civilization for hundreds of years — it means what is not tied down to a specific point of view or bias, what cannot be assigned personal value, what is consequently above the vicissitudes of human nature. The objective scientific experiment is verifiable and duplicatable; it is without history. It is how we know the world based on a particular type of relationship between hypothesis and evidence-gathering, deductive and inductive logic.

One example: to study and understand the phenomenon of memory, people are given rows of nonsense syllables to memorize like PNB, MHI, TYI, FOU. Observations about "long-" and "short-term" memory are taken from the results of these experiments. Generalizations are made from them about how one learns, and consequently, *how one is best taught*. This test is a model of scientific objectivity. It examines memory in an unbiased way because the material doesn't relate to any of the tested subjects' preconceptions. The syllables are detached, general, completely removed from personal meaning, from everyday life; therefore, theoretically, in this way memory as an objective phenomenon can be measured apart from individual association. In my freshman year of college it was compulsory to "volunteer" for one of these experiments. I can personally verify "subjects" have trouble memorizing nonsense syllables — which should come as no surprise, since we are not often called on to memorize things that make absolutely no sense and are completely irrelevant to us. It might, in fact, be fairly argued that all the experiment tests, and tests quite well, is the process by which people learn nonsense syllables, or if you must generalize, how people memorize completely irrelevant material. The problem is the results of this type of experiment are used in making practical decisions about education and learning.

This type of test has gained notoriety because of the controversy over I.Q. and similar tests used to "track" students, directing them into trades or further academic options — in many cases permanently determining their future. The I.Q. test — a supposedly "objective" examination of a subject's ability to learn — has turned out to be more objectionable than objective. The most accepted solution to the short-comings of I.Q. tests has been to make the testing procedure even more abstract — correctly trying to eliminate the strong class, race, and gender bias of the examination, but overlooking the fact that *class bias, cultural prejudice and sexism can be built into procedures as well as subject matter*. A better solution would be to call the whole process into question and test instead to determine what the student has learned, finding out other information through personal interviewing, counseling and much more individualized procedures — which admittedly take more time and cost more money. Unless, of course, the real reason for the test is to siphon out "undesirables" to begin with.

It is interesting to note that many of the sections used on the standard I.Q. test (for example, the analogy and logical number sequences) are the same tests used to predict competence in computer programming skills. Not because the future programmers are being tested for their I.Q., but because these tests measure how well one manipulates mathematical concepts.

The basic flaw in the reasoning underlying all these tests is that we, as living beings relating to other living beings, do not speak to each other as disembodied mouths. If we do, it is perceived as either intentionally or unconsciously evasive or hostile. Our language is not composed of nonsense syllables, or at least it isn't as long as we can relate to what we're talking about. If our language "fails" us, loses meaning, it is because we have failed ourselves. It is not language that loses meaning, we are the ones who lose meaning — as individuals, as a collective.

To examine language as a disembodied, abstract structure, looking at it for the meaning in our lives, is like looking at a gun and asking why *it* makes *us* killers.

As living human beings, we both speak and listen to each other from our own history; we relate to each other from our own point of view, our own place. We are not a scientific control group, hermetically sealed; we are a living community of complex, purposeful, creative individuals (whether individual be defined as a person, culture, community) who live a varied and multi-layered experience. We speak out of a certain space, from a certain time. And sometimes it takes a kind of "suspended disbelief" to hear each other at all — a "stopping" of our own world, of how we are used to experiencing and understanding things, to literally *admit* another's existence, particularly if that existence differs radically from our own.

It takes a suspension of logic to allow two wholly different conceptions — conceptions that might or might not prove to be mutually exclusive — to exist in the same place, at the same time. It takes security, and it takes good faith. We must trust that our world will not be attacked or irrevocably shattered. We must be open to the other. To do this, to fully understand and trust ourselves; we must have information that is more than words, that is action, motivation, feeling, connection.

It is easier to "suspend disbelief" when relating to art, since we are not confronting a living being, and consequently, feel less threatened, more in control — even if that is also an illusion. Because if art reaches deeply enough, or is alien enough, it can pose the same questions, excite the same fears.

To be able to temporarily suspend our own prevailing assumptions, our own reality, knowing our world may never be the same again. Perhaps, at bottom, that is precisely what all learning, all growth, questioning, all communication is really about.

The Ethics of Expediency

Each century, each generation, each nation, culture, sub-culture, group, each individual bases their view of reality on certain sets of unstated and often unconscious assumptions, assumptions that determine much about what and how we choose. The choices of the scientist seemingly are based solely on a set of standards of measurement and procedure aimed at achieving whatever goal the particular experiment involves. Beyond strict adherence to these professional standards, there is no other standard *per se* in scientific research, since only regulations appropriate to the formal aspects of an experiment or hypothesis are allowable as objective. Other than that, like any other citizen, scientists have to obey the laws of the particular society in which they live — kidnapping someone for an experiment, for example, would either be the subject of a Grade B movie or would subject the offender to criminal prosecution. In fact, the needs of science often come in conflict with the laws of society.

However, it can be argued that modern science actually is based on a set of ethical assumptions as well as professional procedures and that *these values are expected to tacitly parallel those of the class in control of the society in which the scientist lives.* Modern science and scientific theory, although nominally cut off from a wider social perspective are nonetheless, in their procedures as well as their aims, governed by a specific set of values, an ethic. And, in our society, that ethic is an ethic of expediency.

The word "expediency" is defined by *Webster's New World Dictionary* as "the doing or consideration of what is of selfish use or advantage rather than what is right or just..." An ethics of expediency is a set of values based solely on personal gain, on achieving the end set regardless of any other consideration.

Our most modern tool is the computer. The computer is a multiplicity of machines depending on its use. It is a game, a word-processor, a clerical aid, an instrument for saving lives, a weapon. The computer, by itself, can do nothing. The assumptions on which its programming is based are those belonging to the architects of the system — the people who design and program it. And, of course, those they design it for. There is always a factor of unpredictability built into a complex system; some of the larger systems seem to be extremely unpredictable. But the computer is dependent on its designers, users, its human base. It is a thing. To believe that the "decisions" or conclusions reached by using a computer are "objective," (any more than science itself is "objective," because it uses a mathematical language) is one of the great and greatly usable myths of our modern age.

What this new technology means to us in practical terms in a context where the prevailing ethic is expediency and the motive is profit is not abstract. In the business community, it is reflected in the presence of workers who will never go back to their old jobs because business has been trying for years to find a way to circumvent the unions in order to fire workers and automate. It is reflected in workers who will never be re-trained for new jobs because people can be found to replace them at lower wages — which is precisely what happened when the typesetting industry became computerized. It is reflected in the generation of a new kind of factory worker, the clerical assembly line, not working directly with production, not even controlling it indirectly through a keyboard, but hooked into a central computer somewhere, performing a routine task — the new "piece-work."

In a political sense, the new technology is also reflected in the increasing disintegration of the United States as a privileged preserve, as more and more international mergers take place and business goes world-wide with a vengeance — and the attendant

153

flagrant disregard for that part of the population not considered "useful." And along with this, the lowering of the work force's standard of living, not because of "equal distribution of wealth," because of greed.

The combination of information theory with behavioral psychology and computer technology is sure to have an enormous effect on education. What could be beneficial will turn into a nightmare if, instead of using the new technology constructively to stimulate both the development of logical thought processes (problem solving) *and* creativity, and teaching more effectively by using, for example, some of the new techniques combining computers and video, computer technology is used to screen information reaching students, to eliminate the teacher *and other students* (the presence of the classroom) altogether, and to further alienate a generation of students already "turned-off" to their world.

The effects of the combination of information theory, computer technology and biology are impossible to predict. Genetic engineering and chemical experimentation could well turn into the next atomic debacle — making the atom bomb and nuclear power plants look tame in retrospect.

These are only a few examples. The point is that *without a political (both theoretical and practical) understanding of the new technology and the ideas behind it, we will not be able to quickly enough delineate areas of important political concern* and the resulting mystification of the "new age of information" will mean that computer technology, instead of freeing us from dangerous and deadly work and enriching our lives, will become a powerful instrument of oppression.

Logic, math, the computer, communication techniques, (even language), are neither positive nor negative. In themselves, they are nothing. They are tools, and as tools they have no objectivity. They are objects. They are always used by *someone* for *something*.

Tools are political instruments, and they must be politically perceived.

The Computer as Metaphor

In modern terms, information theory fits neatly into a schema in which creativity is subsumed under problem-solving and metaphor becomes synonymous with analogue. And, regardless of their protestations to the contrary, it is perhaps here that the greatest danger from theorists of the new technology lies — by the clouding of these distinctions, the computer itself becomes a metaphor for our thought process and, ultimately, the way we inhabit our world. Reality shifts from information we receive from a living environment to the secondary patterns of the computer screen.

It is interesting that the philosopher most immediately conjured up in texts on information theory, artificial intelligence and related subjects, and even specifically quoted is Aristotle — an Aristotle albeit cut off from his own context and re-interpreted through Twentieth century eyes. In any case, while Aristotle is cited because of his denial of Plato's ideal world of universals and his declaration that only through the particulars of this world can knowledge be gained, underneath Aristotle's reasoning is an abstract formalism just as great as Plato's. Aristotle's abstractions are biologically based; they are grounded in living relationships rather than on things, on motion rather than stasis, on generalizations from the natural world rather than abstract ideas. But to use his arguments against Platonic "idealism" to prop up information theory is misleading at best — first, because Plato has nothing to do with the mechanism which information theory cavalierly claims to supersede; and second, because the mathematical formulations behind information theory are easily as idealistic as anything Plato ever dreamed of.

To speak of purpose built into nature — even if it is a materialist's version (without conscious intent) — is scientifically suspect at best. Perhaps the main reason Aristotle has been dredged up again is the authority and respectability that can be gained by citing his theories of causality, which in a somewhat truncated form fit nicely into this updated argument of "creation from design."

Aristotle's theory of the "final cause," of potentiality and actuality — within the acorn, for example, is the oak tree waiting to be actualized — seems to fit perfectly with DNA coding; in fact, with the whole idea of coding. His discussion of multiple causes: formal, efficient, final, material defines complexity in opposition to the single cause-effect relationship of mechanism. His abstracting of logical relationships from activity and his tenacity in categorizing also lend themselves to the information theorist's agenda.

Also important is the idea common in the ancient world that art is craft, that the end must be kept in mind from the inception of the creative process — which is, indeed, a selecting out with an end in view. For Aristotle plot was the most important element of tragedy; action, as a set of relationships that could be reconstructed, was the play. Action that had a logic that was in place from the first moment of the writing of the play, even though the details remained to be worked through.

The tie-in with computer technology should begin to clear. If the structure, the logic, of a plot can be put into mathematical terminology, a predicate calculus, there is nothing to stop one from programming it into the computer and finally discovering what the creative process is really all about. The type of logical process and creative selection we're talking about is, after all, an extremely complex but certainly determinable type of problem-solving. Many experiments, in fact, *are* now being done with computers tracing the development of plotting, following exactly this pattern.

Besides which any of our thoughts, feelings, fears, visions that can be put into language should in theory be able to be translated and programmed into a computer and be reducible finally to mathematical terms — their secrets revealed, their structure laid bare.

Like the human being, the computer is a symbol manipulator, and words are symbols. Anything that can be said can be coded. Although our specific thoughts are different, in the structure of our thinking apparatus, we are ostensibly the same. Some theorists even believe if a thought cannot be expressed in language, it can't be formulated at all.

156

The conviction is that as our skill with these new computer techniques grows, our ability to understand our own thought processes, our own creativity, will also grow.

It is true that literature uses words and through literature even emotion and highly complex ideas and experiences can be captured — but what does that mean? Is the literary metaphor really no more than symbol substitution? Is it really the same as analogies used in computer programs or I.Q. tests?

Even though literature utilizes words, those words can be non-verbal. The poetic metaphor is more than logical manipulation; its purpose is to combine terms and construct new relations *from the full being of the poetic experience.* It is a unity — produced through creative use of language — of smell and sound and touch and sight and thought, as well as problems, questions, hopes, dreams, lemons, sweetness, the red convertible, my mother's voice, a dictionary, B flat, a headache, a strand of red-brown hair. It is individual and unique. A point in time — 10 o'clock or the 1st of May. It is poignant, alive, *and it can be transmitted,* empathized with, understood.

It is not reducible to a paraphrase or mathematical equation. It cannot be plotted. It is not repeatable. It happens only once.

Complexity doesn't mean adding layers and layers of complication, moving in numerous directions along the same plane. *The new technology is not complex; it is complicated.* A computer, a television set, a telephone, an automobile, a mill to grind grain all have one thing in common — they are machines.

What McLuhan was looking for in his new electronic media has been here all the time. It can be reached with *any* medium — glance, gesture, music, words, paint.

The creative metaphor works because it brings things together that are *different in kind.* It works not only because of surface technique, but because it reaches from what is open in the poet to what is open in the person who hears the poem. It touches what is beneath the surface. To leave that out is to misunderstand what a poem is. Our world is rich and varied and cannot be reduced to a set of ciphers, or even to an unlimited number of plots.

From the beginnings of our recorded history, there have been warnings about the dangers of making and worshipping images. Of mistaking the image for what it represents.

The car is not our legs; the stick, our arms; the camera, our eyes — and the computer is not our brain. If we keep defining ourselves by our constructs instead of the living complexity we are; if we continue to view experience as a problem to be solved, the outside world as a manipulable pattern; if we continue to lose ourselves in machines we think we can control, that give us the illusion of certitude and power; if we continue to refuse responsibility for our own choices, throwing the onus back on inanimate matter, we give up our own humanity and any possibility of real and lasting change.

BIBLIOGRAPHY

Margaret Boden, *Artificial Intelligence and Natural Man*. Basic Books.

Jeremy Campbell, *Grammatical Man*. Simon and Schuster.

Michael L.Dertouzos and Joel Moses (eds.) *The Computer Age: A Twenty-Year View*. M.I.T. Press.

Lila L. Gatlin. *Information Theory & The Living System*. Columbia University Press.

Martin Heidegger, *The Question Concerning Technology and Other Essays*. (translation & introduction by William Lovitt.) Harper Colophon Books.

Marshall McLuhan, *Understanding Media*. A Mentor Book.

Joseph Weizenbaum. *Computer Power and Human Reason: From Judgment to Calculation*.

THE ABC OF MADNESS:
The Legacy of Derrida

strange...not to interpret roses, and other things that promise so much, in
terms of a human future: ...and to lay aside even one's proper name like
a broken toy.
— Rainer Marie Rilke, *Duino Elegies*

But that the key should be left behind — at the window — the key in the
sunlight — to the living — that can take that slice of light in hand
— and turn the door — and look back...
— Allen Ginsberg, *Kaddish*

IF I COULD TURN YOU ON,
IF I COULD DRIVE YOU OUT OF YOUR
WRETCHED MIND,
IF I COULD TELL YOU
I WOULD LET YOU KNOW.
— The Living Theater, *Paradise Now*

It is a crisp fall day in 1959. In front of a large, attentive
English class at the University of California at Berkeley, a
professor noted for his literary achievements leans forward and
proclaims in a loud voice with appropriate hand gestures that
literary creativity in the United States is dead — the true creative
spirit is now to be found in literary criticism, in people like Allen
Tate and Yvor Winters. As he speaks, across the bay in San
Francisco an unparalleled "renaissance" in American poetry and
art is going on literally under his nose.

To this day I remember that scene vividly. I have long
forgotten the professor's name, but his words reverberate as I
read the work of Jacques Derrida and the underlying "news"
implicit in it that the original work has all been done and what is
appropriate at this particular time is deconstruction, commentary,
collage.

159

Today there are many Derridas. There is Derrida himself, the innovator, the commentator, the Talmudist, the philosopher. There are the multitudes of Derridas seen through the eyes of his interpreters: the students of philosophy, literary critics, artists, art critics and historians, intellectuals. There is the Derrida of deconstruction and Post-Modernism.

With Derrida, a curious thing has happened to criticism, the field where his impact is perhaps most felt in this country. The critic has been raised to a hitherto unheard of status, beyond that of the creator of the particular text interpreted, beyond even the status of creative artist. Derridian criticism is philosophy in its broadest sense. As Freud analyzed not only the narrative but the configuration of the world of his patients and finally the structure of human consciousness (including the unconscious), Derridian critics interpret the world that the narrative of the text, and finally the text itself, inhabits. They re-place the text with (within) the narrative of life.

As a result of this marriage of psychoanalysis, philosophy and art criticism, the contemporary Derridian becomes not only the interpreter, but the purveyor of the world of the artist, whose works depend now not only on a certain style but on the world view that goes along with it. A world view increasingly reflecting an *innate* undersurface of chaos and violence thinly masked by the genial surface of civilized society. A world view presented not as a reflection of contemporary society, changing and changeable, but as human nature. This conceptualization and the stylistic devices it generates have become in fashionable intellectual and artistic circles the hallmark of true artistic sophistication, and any other perspective is dismissed as at best naive and primitive, at worse, sentimental and romantic.

If it is our limits that define us, those silent places beyond which one cannot go that finally circumscribe what one can know about the world and our place in it, the best place to start an examination of Derrida is by examining the limits he sets himself.

"where you want to get to......"

In *Alice in Wonderland* when Alice, lost and hopelessly confused by the seemingly endless and contradictory paths of Wonderland, asks the Cheshire-Cat which way she "ought to go," the Cat advises her, "That depends on where you want to get to."[1] Alice, even though told finally that no matter which direction she goes in she is bound to get "somewhere," still has the sneaking suspicion she is, in fact, getting nowhere. In "The time of a thesis: punctuations," Jacques Derrida, confronting a similar dilemma, traces/defends the development of his thought through what he sees as three specific periods — this, in answer to a seemingly simple and straight-forward reaction to a paper of Derrida's by Jean Hyppolite: "I really do not see where you are going."[2]

While Derrida's first reaction to Hyppolite's criticism is:

> I then thought that knowing where one is going may doubtless help in orienting one's thought, but that it has never made anyone take a single step, quite the opposite in fact. What is the good of knowing where one knows oneself to be going and where one knows that one is destined to arrive?[3]

He soon realizes that neither chance nor his own intellectual manipulation is involved:

> But there's always Necessity. The figure I wanted recently to call Necessity with the capital of a proper noun, and Necessity says that one must always yield, that one has always to go where it calls. At the risk of never arriving.[4]

So there *is* a destination (trace/gap/*difference*) that draws one to it, but it is *its own place,* unable to be manipulated, controlled. Not *"Where* are you going...," where are you being enticed/tantalized, even the "where" a misnomer — the "where" might well be "no-where," the lack of place, the space beyond or between, the abyss of Nietzsche, the Freudian unconscious, the "horror" at the "heart of darkness," a place "I in fact know enough about it to think, with a certain terror, that things there are not going very well and that, all things considered, it would be better not to go there at all."[5]

This leads directly to Derrida's central enterprise echoing Ezra Pound more than thirty years earlier in the *ABC of Reading,* as Derrida conceptualizes the question which will provide the transition into the second period of his work, the period in which Antonine Artaud, actor, playwright, creator of the Theater of Cruelty, surfaces as a major focus:

> What is literature? And first of all what is it 'to write'? How is it that the fact of writing can disturb the very question 'what is?' and even 'what does it mean?'...*saying otherwise*...when and how does an inscription become literature and what takes place when it does? To what and to whom is this due?[6]

So Derrida's project is based not on a thesis, a hypothesis, but on a question, Necessity, yearning, a "fascination," "desire," "uneasiness," "the whole ungraspable paradox of the trace."

Derrida's will ideally be a "strategy without any finality,"[7] an endless trail. Because what he is about, *or says he is about,* is continuously testing limits, going beyond borders, breaking new ground. Even though it will turn out that his project is defined finally by a self-imposed limit beyond which he will not pass:

> My interest for these more or less visible framework structures, for these limits, these margin effects or these paradoxes of edging continued to relate to the same question: how is it that philosophy finds itself inscribed, rather than itself inscribing itself, within a space which it seeks but is unable to control, a space which opens out onto another which is no longer even *its* other.[8]

Artaud & Madness/The Second Stage

During the years from "about 1963 to 1968,"[9] his middle or second period, Antonine Artaud, poet/madman, is a more significant figure for Derrida than Sigmund Freud, scientist/observer/doctor of the mad. It is Artaud, for the moment, who directs, to whom Derrida's attention is directed. But is the focus of Derrida's attention Artaud's madness or his art?

Artaud's breaching of boundaries led finally to his confinement. It meant not a furthering, but a loss of freedom. Where exactly is the "slice of light" framed by the bars of Artaud's cell that will serve as Derrida's key in his project of pushing against, breaking against, breaching the edges, the boundaries that confine philosophical discourse, that border the

162

epoch of Western metaphysics within which we are currently imprisoned?

Derrida uses Artaud and particularly Artaud's work, *The Theater and its Double,* as the center of his attack on the epoch of the metaphysical, the rule of Logos, the "Name of the Father," the totalitarian regime of the Logo-phonocentric monotheistic God in which we find ourselves. An epoch of words, phonemes, *the freezing of "speech" on the page.* Opposed to speech, to the written *work,* Derrida juxtaposes "writing," which is ever new because it is fluid, changeable and changing.

Artaud, pivotal, is a wheel the hub of which radiates many spokes. A wheel which rests restlessly on the ground. A ground which makes its mark on the wheel and each moment as it is passed/past disappears. A wheel which, like a madman itself, speaks in constant dialogue with that ground, as Derrida speaks in his work of that period to Artaud.

It is this ground which provides the base/basis for Derrida's "a-thesis," and it is Artaud, in a passage from "The Theater of Cruelty and the Closure of Representation," who "speaks" first.

> ...all words, once spoken are dead and function only at the moment when they are uttered, ...a form, once it has served, cannot be used again and asks only to be replaced by another. ...the theater is the only place in the world where a gesture, once made, can never be made the same way twice.[10]

In order to break through the limitations of spoken or written language as we know it, through the limitations of our particular epoch, an epoch characterized by the investigation of *Being,* (whether "Being" be understood as the human's innate identity or as a monotheistic, all-encompassing divinity in order to get at least some glimpse of, *insight into,* if not to get *inside of,* the "disappearance" of any alternative, of what came before, of what will go beyond, to identify the "trace," we have to find an instrument, a "way in" or at least "out." The enemy of our investigation is compulsive repetition, representation, all that repeats, doubles back on itself — the principle of Thanatos, death, as expressed most succinctly by Freud in his work, *Beyond the Pleasure Principle.*

The creation by naming sets this process in motion. — as the Judeo-Christian God created the world through the phoneme, through "logos," the word, order, logic which, as it was aspirated/spoken out took form and brought the world into *being* through His alphabet, His voice shaping the letters of Hebrew, the sacred language of abstract form.

To understand how Derrida juxtaposes the concept of "writing" with that of "naming," to see why Artaud is so important to him, it is first necessary to ask: "What indeed *is*, for him, in a name. What is he acting toward/against?

> For what his (Artaud's) howls promise us, articulating themselves under the headings of *existence, flesh, life, theater, cruelty* is the meaning of an art prior to madness *and* the work, an art which no longer yields works, an artist's existence which is no longer a route or an experience that give access to something other than itself..."[11]

For Derrida, Artaud shows us the route away from the art *work* (art *object*), from the written word (literature), to writing, the creative imagination, that place before/beyond separation (individuation/objectification). That place prior to the separation of the artist/subject from the art/object.

For many of Derrida's contemporaries a name is neither a label placed on something already there or a concept already in the mind prior to the existence of the physical object. The act of naming brings the object into being, it literally *objectifies* it. An infant first begins to form ideas of objects through being presented with them in terms of language, in terms of usage, in terms of *names*. For example, a toy (round, soft, bounces) becomes a *ball* and the "attributes of that object are subsumed and taken for granted under that name... The 'name' does not 'stand for' the object, it *is* the object. The 'name' is, in fact, that means by which the multiple attributes (soft, round, etc.) *become* an object."[12] And it follows that by self or communal naming, the subject individuates/objectifies her/himself.

> The word, far from being the mere sign of objects and meanings, inhabits things and is the vehicle of meanings. Thus speech, in the speaker, does not translate ready-made thought, but accomplishes it.[13]

The quandary that this produces is that as "an object is brought into perspective, the field in which it rests recedes into the background."[14] French phenomenologist Merleau-Ponty describes, in his essay on Cezanne, the painter catching the edges of the object as he/it constructs itself in the early morning light.[15]

Both the object and the objectifier (subject) under this interpretation are seen as constructions. To de-construct *being* (the name, the object), as well as *Being* (the Name/Namer, the subject), allows us, if not to glimpse the (back)ground, at least to open and re-open our own options, to rename, re-construct. Or if that is not possible, at any rate to *under*stand where it *is* we stand. If, finally, we are not even able to recognize, glimpse, face the truth, at least we will know the lie.

For Derrida, any notion that speech forms thought is a basic part of the lie, no matter how accurate an analysis of "naming" might be. It is not speech, not the written word (the reproduction of the phonemes of speech) but writing (what is beyond/behind speech before it is separated out, divided, dislocated) which forms the real background that must be brought into focus, recognized, re-turned.

Frederick Nietzsche, in some ways closely akin to Artaud, also chooses theater as the art form which most enables human beings to glimpse the hidden reality behind our illusion of order and reason. Nietzsche sees individuation as a necessary "evil" for which art "is the joyous hope." The Apollonian (individuation, form, shape) for him is subservient to the powerful intoxication of the Dionysian: *"Excess* revealed itself as truth. Contradiction, the bliss born of pain, spoke out from the very heart of nature."[16] But without the Apollonian, the Dionysian is impossible even to glimpse. To partake in the ancient rites, to become one with the primal unity, the life force (which is the Dionysian) is to give way to complete intoxication, to lose consciousness, to forget. The Apollonian and Dionysian are redeemed in each other:

> The Greek knew and felt the terror and horror of existence. That he might endure this terror at all, he had to interpose between himself and life the radiant dream-birth of the Olympians...[17]

But Nietzsche adds:

> The more clearly I perceive in nature those omnipotent art impulses, and in them an ardent self impelled to the metaphysical assumption that the truly existent primal unity, eternally suffering and contradictory, also needs the rapturous vision, the pleasurable illusion, for its continuous redemption.[18]

and it is here that he parts company with Derrida who rejects the "metaphysical" theory of the primal unity, of the oneness of underlying reality, of *Being*. The breaking of individuation is not, as in Nietzsche, accompanied by the "augury of a restored oneness."[19] And here is where the danger of madness arises. Touching the "trace" is to risk the loss of individuation, of self, in a much more critical sense than in Nietzsche, because the loss is neither temporary nor redeemable. It puts even the *illusion* of self into question. Opposed to the Apollonian is not a primal oneness, but a multiplicity, a chaos, which makes a lie of the whole concept of "unity" in either human beings or the divine.

Nietzsche, for Derrida, is still caught in self, in *Being*, in oneness, even if it is terrifying, horrific, cruel. Nietzsche is still caught in the law, (order) of the Creator, whether or not he pronounces Him dead. For Nietzsche the visible is a shield; the primal unity is represented by music which can transcend the limitations of the seen. For Derrida there is no primal unity, representation is a lie, and it is precisely the ascendancy of the ear that must be broken. The way is not beyond the visual, the visible, but through it. The tyranny of form is not restricted to the visual; music also has shape, rhythm has form profoundly constraining, as physical as visual form. As Artaud says in *The Theater and its Double*:

> Furthermore, when we speak the word 'life,' it must be understood we are not referring to life as we know it from its surface of fact, but that fragile, functioning center which forms never reach. And if there is still one hellish, truly accursed thing in our time, it is our artistic dallying with forms, instead of being like victims burnt at the stake, signaling through the flames.[20]

The way out of the metaphysical is *via* the body, is by passage into the *depths* of the physical, not away from it. Nowhere does

Artaud state this as clearly as in "Van Gogh / The Man Suicided by Society," when he says, talking about the "basic human schism' between Van Gogh and Gauguin:

> I believe that Gauguin thought that an artist should seek the symbol, the myth, enlarge the things of life and raise them to the status of the myth,while Van Gogh believed that the myth should be deduced from the most earthly things in life.
> And I think he was damned right...[21]

Van Gogh is not a representational artist, he does not represent nature, he does not use nature to symbolize some hidden reality, *he goes to the heart of the actual* — he "de-constructs" it.

> Van Gogh is a painter because he re-collected nature as if he had re-perspired it and made it sweat, made it spurt forth in luminous beams onto his canvas, in monumental clusters of colors, the secular crushing of elements, the fearful elementary pressure of apostrophes, stripes, commas, bars, and we can no longer believe, after him, that the natural aspects of nature are not made up of these things...[22]

Or, as Derrida puts it,

> Rigid with rage against God, convulsed with anger against the work, Artaud does not renounce salvation... For, by definition, the only thing that is not subject to commentary is the life of the body, the living flesh whose integrity, opposed to evil and death, is maintained by the theater.[23]

It is not the spirit, the soul, but the individual body that is singular, unique. If Artaud is rigid with rage against God, so is Derrida. If "the theater of cruelty expels God from the stage,"[24] if the "stage is theological for as long as it is dominated by speech, by a will to speech, by the layout of a primary logos that governs it from a distance,"[25] that does not mean the end of the divine. The affirmation of the theater of cruelty is that *only by expelling God can the divine be understood.*

> A new epiphany of the supernatural and the divine must occur within cruelty. And not despite but thanks to the eviction of God and the destruction of the theater's theological machinery. The divine has been ruined by God. That is to say, by man, who in permitting himself to be usurped from his own birth, became man by polluting the divinity of the divine.[26]

The Hebrew/Cabalist Creator, *Ain Suph*, G-d, the forbidden-to-be-spoken Name of the Father, who created by the word, each letter of the Hebrew alphabet bringing another part of creation into being, not only the "logos" of St. John, but the very form, shape of the Hebrew letter, the Cabalistic mystical act of creation, the speaking of the magical Yod-Heh-Vau-Heh, the most secret name of names. The Gnostic God/creator Jehovah, Yahweh, the demonic creator of earth and human beings, tormentor of Blake and Durrell and Artaud who must be circumvented for divinity to be claimed. The original Creator/Author, "I am that I am," law giver, the eternal "one," the giver of the sacred "Book (of laws)." *Being*. To see whose face is to die or go mad.

> But what if the Book was only, in all senses of the word, an *epoch* of Being... If the form of the book was no longer to be the model of meaning?... The dissimulation of an older or younger writing, from an age other than the age of the book, the age of grammar, the age of everything announced under the heading of the meaning of Being? The dissimulation of a still illegible writing?[27]

Would this be madness? No, because madness as we know it is possible *only in relation* to Being:

> The radical illegibility of which we are speaking is not irrationality... Prior to the book (in the nonchronological sense), original illegibility is therefore the very possibility of the book and within it, of the ulterior and eventual opposition of "rationalism" and "irrationalism."[28]

Beyond "Being & Madness"

Is there any way to be more specific about this "radical illegibility?" Is there any *tangible* "trace" of it to be found? Derrida carefully makes it prior in a "nonchronological" sense which means *beyond*, not *before*. It is here that he finds in both Freud and Artaud a key — Freud in his use of hieroglyph to interpret dreams:

> If we reflect that the means of representation in dreams are principally visual images and not words, we shall see that it is even more important to compare dreams with a system of writing than with a language. In fact the interpretation of dreams is completely analogous to the decipherment of an ancient pictographic script such as Egyptian hieroglyphs. [29]

But Artaud goes even further. The Theater of Cruelty is a syntax of *living* hieroglyphs — communicating on many perceptual levels (visual, sensory, plastic), each repetition, unique. In the *Theater and its Double* Artaud writes and Derrida quotes:

> 'Once aware of this language in space, language of sounds, cries, lights, onomatopoeia, the theater must organize it into veritable hieroglyphs, with the help of characters and objects, and make use of their symbolism and interconnections in relation to all organs and on all levels.'[30]

The point is not the elimination of spoken language, "but of giving words approximately the importance they have in dreams."[31] The living presence, the uniqueness of each performance adds gestural significance, restores meaning. The theater is rid of the creator/author, of the written text. A model for going "beyond" *Being* is secured.

Artaud relies heavily on Balinese theater and on Japanese Noh drama as models. Both Balinese and Noh theater rely on traditionally shared symbols on the part of their audience and performers. In "Two-Way Mirrors," Ron Jenkins describes the response of a Balinese audience "to a performance that links them to their ancestors in a whirl of color, sound and emotion."[32] During the performance, the individual actor, the *individuality* of the actor, is hidden behind a mask, allowing the actor to assume roles that bridge the particular with the universal, the mundane with the archetypal image. This is the power of Balinese theater. It depends on a signifier with a specific, static, universal meaning. It is built on a symbolism which is immutable, universal, not one that is never "in the same place twice." It is ironic in this context that Artaud champions Van Gogh's arguments against Gauguin's use of the symbol in painting.

Furthermore, Artaud does not believe in "the theater collective." *The Living Theater*, the theater that comes closest to actually putting his theories into practice, would be dismissed by him — because they are a collective — as anarchists. Which, of course, they are! But lacking set symbols, who creates and supervises this formal, unambiguous theater of Artaud's? *Is it possible that the tyranny of the author will be replaced only by another tyranny — that of the director? Or, in Derrida's case, the tyranny of the author with that of the critic or commentator?*

Artaud leaves no room for any art form except theater (with the possible exception of dance.) In a quote Derrida cites that could be interpreted as very close to Derrida's own feelings about written works, Artaud states: "We should get rid of our superstitious valuation of text and written poetry. Written poetry is worth reading once, and then should be destroyed."[33]

What about painted paintings? They are as much "names" as poetry and other textual material. If they are not, neither are poems. What about Van Gogh's paintings? Should they be looked at once and then destroyed? Poems or paintings don't have to continually change to retain their uniqueness — that is one of the attributes of art, that it leaves room, space, within itself, both for the viewer and for time itself. With each viewer, at each moment, in each context, the work of art changes.

Besides which, all the arts, not only theater, have their methods of creating an environment of "sounds, cries, lights," bringing the apparatus of all the senses into their limited space — this is the challenge of whatever art context you create within. Through his use of what he called "expressive color" Van Gogh writes he wanted people to smell, to taste, to experience the raw textures delineated by his work.

However, Artaud does look outside traditional "Western" culture (meaning the Western European tradition) in his search for new forms, a new theater, in a very intensive and thorough way — besides his writing on the Japanese, Balinese and Tibetan cultures, his work on Mexican tradition is particularly interesting. Derrida, however, abruptly stops at this point. In fact, if you only knew Artaud through Derrida, you would never even guess the extent to which Artaud's explorations into other cultures, including extensive traveling, influenced his work.

The Third Stage: Back to Freud & Beyond

Given the complexity of Derrida's reasoning and references it is hard not to wind up with more questions than you started out with, and one of the most important must be, does Derrida really want to change philosophy, to "de-construct" it in order to "re-construct" it, as much as he wants to provide a commentary on its texts, experimenting with language *within* the given tradition?

As an epigraph to "Violence and Metaphysics An Essay on the Thought of Emmanuel Levinas," he uses a quote by Matthew Arnold that accurately sums up his own dilemma:

> Hebraism and Hellenism, — between these two points of influence moves our world. At one time it feels more powerfully the attraction of one of them, at another time of the other; and it ought to be, though it never is, evenly and happily balanced between them[34]

Arnold writes, "...moves *our* world." But in "Freud and the Scene of Writing," Derrida changes that "our" to "the": "...logo-phonocentrism is not a philosophical or historical error which the history of philosophy, of the West, that is, of *the* world, would have rushed into pathologically, but is rather a necessary, and necessarily finite, movement and structure..."[35] The history of *Western philosophy* is the history of the world only if you believe *the history of the West* is the history of the world. There are and always have been *other* histories. Artaud explores them. Derrida does not. He doesn't even explore them in relationship to Artaud. The fact that even though Derrida is so intensely critical of the content and insularity of Western thought, he never steps beyond it, has wide ranging repercussions, particularly given the popularity of his ideas and their influence on art criticism and art. *It also produces the single most telling limit on his work — a limit which is self-inflicted.* In the words of Cornel West, writing on "Black Culture and Postmodernism":

> Derrida's own marginal status as Algerian (a special type of French colonial subject) and a Jew may indeed lead him to highlight the transgressive and disruptive aspects of Nietzsche and Heidegger, Mallarme and Artaud. Yet his project remains a thoroughly Eurocentric and modernist one.[36]

Is this the real reason for Derrida's abruptly turning at the end of his exegesis on Artaud from the ideas of the man to the man himself, from an exposition of Artaud's ideas to a statement of the impossibility of their implementation? Is this the reason for Derrida's turn from Artaud, the actor, madman, to Freud, the

171

observer of the mad? Is this the reason that from now on he will concentrate on commentary, exegesis, deconstruction, the *way he speaks* rather than *what he has to say?*

The reason Derrida gives for re-turning (turning back) is that he has now found the limit beyond which *no one* can go:

> The "grammar" of the theater of cruelty, of which he (Artaud) said that it is "to be found," will always remain the inaccessible limit of a representation which is not repetition...[37]

The inaccessible limit which means the outer, not the inner edge.

> To think the closure of representation is to think the tragic: not as the representation of fate, but as the fate of representation. Its gratuitous and baseless necessity.[38]

Does Derrida, now detached, now the observer, attribute Artaud's madness to his "thinking the closure of representation?" Not only because of the tragic aspect of realizing the necessity of representation, but in the "how" of that realization? Derrida contends that to go beyond *being*, one risks the experience of that other side of *being*, madness. *He posits madness itself as the outer limit of* being, *what keeps one from truly going beyond.* In "Cognito and the History of Madness," Derrida writes:

> To define philosophy as the attempt-to-say-the-hyperbole is to confess — and philosophy is perhaps this gigantic confession — that by virtue of the historical enunciation through which philosophy tranquilizes itself and excludes madness, philosophy also betrays itself (or betrays itself as thought), enters into a crisis and a forgetting of itself that are an essential and necessary period of its movement. I philosophize only in *terror*, but in the *confessed* terror of going mad. The confession is simultaneously, at its *present* moment, oblivion and unveiling, protection and exposure: economy.[39]

Afraid to strike out, to continue, for fear of breaking the barriers of thought, Derrida turns back in on himself, places himself in a ghetto of his own making, setting his own limits, the limits of a world whose time has passed.

It is not crossing the barriers of *being* that caused Artaud's madness. Using Artaud to generalize about art, much less philosophy, is like the now fashionable use of Poe (and Poe's short stories at that) to make wide-ranging generalizations about the nature of poets and poetry.

If there *is* a beyond of *being*, its way is not blocked by madness but by the limits of the tradition that defines it. The risk is not losing your mind but your central position by virtue of birth and personal history, the risk of admitting your own particular history is not the only, perhaps not even the most important one. This is the risk Derrida refuses to take. *Being* and madness are not the only alternatives and there are histories which extend beyond the twin pillars of Greek and Judeo-Christian tradition.

This very day, outside his classroom door, even as Derrida speaks, a new history, *another* kind of art and even philosophy is being drawn, poems and books are being written, paintings and theater and music created. A renaissance based on a history that includes rather than excludes "Third World peoples, women, gays, lesbians."[40] A *creative* renaissance which incorporates deconstruction as a way of recovering history rather than as a substitute for art, which sees art not as a totalitarian construction of an omnipotent creator, but as the expression of the hopes and dreams and aspirations of human beings.

It is hard not to be left finally with an image of Derrida as Talmudic scholar, heeding the exhortations and warnings of the mystic texts and waiting patiently before the gates of The Garden, the limits of *Being*, where it all began. A gate, for him, still guarded by an angel with a flaming sword so that humankind, having eaten of the Tree of Knowledge, will not eat of the Tree of Life and become as gods themselves.

FOOTNOTES

1. Lewis Carroll, *Alice's Adventures in Wonderland & Through the Looking-Glass* (New York: Bantam Books), p.46.
2. Jacques Derrida, "The time of a thesis: punctuations," *Philosophy in France Today*, p.36.
3. Jacques Derrida, "The time of a thesis: punctuations," p.37.
4. *Ibid.*
5. *Ibid.*
6. *Ibid.*pp.37, 38.
7. *Ibid.*p.50.
8. *Ibid.*p.45.
9. *Ibid.*p.40.
10. Jacques Derrida, "The Theater of Cruelty and the Closure of Representation," *Writing and Difference*, p.247.
11. Jacques Derrida, "La parole soufflee," *Writing and Difference*, pp.174, 175..
12. Susan Sherman, "The Category of Language in Merleau-Ponty," p.20.
13. Maurice Merleau-Ponty, *Phenomenology of Perception*, p.178.
14. Susan Sherman, "The Category of Language in Merleau-Ponty," p.5.
15. Maurice Merleau-Ponty, "Cezanne's Doubt," *Sense and Non-Sense*.
16. Friedrich Nietzsche, "Dramatic Reality: from *The Birth of Tragedy*," *Aesthetics, A Critical Anthology*, p. 249.
17. *Ibid.*p.246.
18. *Ibid.*p.248.
19. *Ibid.*p.254.
20. Jacques Derrida, "La parole soufflee," *Writing and Difference*, p. 179.
21. Antonine Artaud, *Artaud Anthology*, p.24.
22. *Ibid.*p.25.
23. Jacques Derrida, "La parole soufflee," *Writing and Difference*, p. 183.
24. Jacques Derrida, "The Theater of Cruelty and the Closure of Representation," *Writing and Difference*, p.235.
25. *Ibid*
26. *Ibid* p. 243.
27. Jacques Derrida, "Edmond Jabes and the Question of the Book," *Writing and Difference*, p.77.
28. *Ibid*
29. Jacques Derrida, "The Theater of Cruelty and the Closure of Representation," *Writing and Difference*, p.241.
30. *Ibid*

31   *Ibid*
32. Ron Jenkins, "Two-Way Mirrors," p.17.
33   Jacques Derrida, "The Theater of Cruelty and the Closure of
     Representation," *Writing and Difference*, p.247.
34   Jacques Derrida, "Violence and Metaphysics An Essay on the
     Thought of Emmanuel Levinas," *Writing and Experience*, p.79.
35   Jacques Derrida, "Freud and the Scene of Writing," *Writing
     and Difference*, p.197. (italics mine)
36. Cornel West, "Black Culture and Postmodernism," p.88.
37. Jacques Derrida, "The Theater of Cruelty and the Closure of
     Representation," *Writing and Difference*, p.248.
38   *Ibid* p. 250.
39. Jacques Derrida, "Cogito and the History of Madness,"
     Writing and Difference, p.62.
40. Cornel West, "Black Culture and Postmodernism," p.88.

BIBLIOGRAPHY

Aristotle. *Aristotle's Poetics*. Translated by S.H. Butcher with an
     introduction by Francis Fergusson. (A Drama Book.) New York:
     Hill and Wang. 1961.

Artaud, Antonin. *Artaud Anthology*. Edited by Jack Hirschman.
     San Francisco: City Lights Books. 1965.

—. *The Theater and its Double*. Translated by Mary Caroline Richards.
     New York: Grove Press. 1958.

Derrida, Jacques. "Cogito and the History of Madness," "Edmond Jabes
     and the Question of the Book," "La Parole soufflee," "Freud and the
     Scene of Writing," "The Theater of Cruelty and the Closure of
     Representation," "Elipsis." *Writing and Difference*. Translated with
     an introduction and notes by Alan Bass. Chicago: The University
     of Chicago Press. 1978.

—. *of Grammatology*. Translated by Gayatri Chakravorty Spivak.
     Baltimore, London: The John Hopkins University Press. 1974, 1976.

—. *The Postcard*. Translated by Alan Bass. Chicago & London:
     The University of Chicago Press. 1987.

—. "The time of a thesis: punctuations." *Philosophy in France Today*. Edited
     by Alan Montefiore. New York: Columbia University Press. 1983.

Handelman, Susan A. *The Slayers of Moses: The Emergence of Rabbinic Interpretation in Modern Literary Theory*. Albany: State University of New York Presses. 1982.

Jenkins, Ron. "Two-Way Mirrors." *Parabola, Volume VI, No. 3. Mask and Metaphor: Role, Imagery, Disguise*. 1981, 1984.

Merleau-Ponty, Maurice. *Phenomenology of Perception*. trans. Colin Smith. London: Routledge & Kegan Paul. New York: The Humanities Press. 1962.

— *Sense and Non-Sense*. trans. Herbert L. Dreyfus & Patricia Allen Dreyfus. Northwestern University Press. 1964.

Nietzsche, Friedrich. "Dramatic reality: from *The Birth of Tragedy*," *Aesthetics: A Critical Anthology*, (eds. George Dickie, R.J. Sclafani. New York: St. Martin's Press. 1977.

Norris, Christopher. *Deconstruction: Theory & Practice*. London, New York: Methuen. 1986.

Pound, Ezra. *A B C of Reading*. (A New Directions Paperback NDP89.) New York: New Directions. 1960.

Sherman, Susan. *The Category of Language in Merleau-Ponty*. Submitted in partial fulfillment of the requirements for the degree of Master of Arts, in the Department of Philosophy, Hunter College, the City University of New York, 1967.

West, Cornel. "Black Culture and Postmodernism," Dia Art Foundation Discussions in Contemporary Culture, Number 4. *Remaking History*. Edited by Barbara Kruger and Phil Mariana. Seattle: Bay Press. 1989.

THE OBSCURE SUBJECT OF DESIRE:
The Despair of Jacques Lacan

...And, making the leap, for whoever is encumbered with the phallus, what is a woman?
   A woman is a symptom.

—Jacques Lacan
"Seminar of 21 January 1975"

Because it is a systematic negation of the other person and a furious determination to deny the other person all attributes of humanity, colonialism forces the people it dominates to ask themselves the question constantly: "In reality, who am I?"

— Frantz Fanon
The Wretched of the Earth

For many political activists one of the lessons of the Sixties was the revelation that economic egalitarianism in and of itself would not solve the problems of racism, sexism and homophobia. The "cultural revolution" of the Fifties and Sixties was one attempt to change peoples' attitudes, but it soon became obvious a more structured approach was needed. Psychoanalysis seemed a perfect solution since it was a science devoted to codifying the laws of psychology, of human behavior, human development, in the same way Marxism had disclosed historical laws regulating economic development.

Jacques Lacan's return to (re-reading of) Freud coupled with his fusion of the theories of Claude Levi-Strauss (who revealed structures underlying cultural constructions) with modern linguistics becomes all the more compelling because it seems to reveal not only a structural psychological matrix but a language, a vocabulary, by which to unravel the unconscious. It seems to disclose a way of cutting through to whatever it is that makes us act in a repetitive and destructive manner and, by implication, change the way we act — even though Lacan himself saw the latter as an advantageous side effect of truth-seeking, healing being for him secondary to activating his patients to confront their psychic condition, both individual and collective.

Lacan is difficult, intentionally so, particularly in his later work. His language is obscure; his analysis complicated and multi-layered. He often gives several explanations for the same phenomena. Conversant with literature, art, Eastern and Western philosophy, which he mixes liberally into his psychoanalytical theories, Lacan works from a cross-disciplinary perspective, making it essential in many instances to go directly to his sources.

What is ironic is in the final analysis Jacques Lacan, who so vehemently denounces the effects on the human psyche of modern technology, turns out to be one of its most eloquent ideologues; Lacan, who so adamantly puts down authoritarianism, constructs an elitist structure in which authoritarianism reaches new heights; Lacan, who acknowledges Freud's ignorance of women, refuses himself to listen. His criticism of the present turns him not toward the future, but to a nostalgia for conservative antiquity. His radical return is a closed circle firmly entrenched in the past, making even more ironic his enthusiastic acceptance and promotion by groups of progressive therapists, Third World intellectuals, feminists and Marxists.

As the other desires, so we "imagine" ourselves to be.

Both Lacan and Marx see the primary causal factors that form individuals as objective and anterior to them — in the case of Marx, economic relationships; in the case of Lacan, the unconscious. For Lacan, the unconscious, although concealed within (the concealment of) the individual subject, is not subjective, it is objective. It is not objective in the Jungian sense of a collective unconscious of mutually shared symbolic imagery, but in a formalist sense, in its syntax (*the unconscious is structured like a language*)[1] as it, in turn, reflects itself dialectically in the syntax of the infant's primary relationship with its mother and father.

> The unconscious is that chapter of my history that is marked by a blank or occupied by a falsehood; it is the censored chapter. But the truth can be rediscovered...the hysterical symptom reveals the structure of a language, and is deciphered like an inscription.[2]

If the unconscious for Lacan is structured like language, death is the parenthesis, the limitation or boundary upon which life is defined. The ability to look into the abyss, to face the fact of a temporal and temporary existence stripped of inherent meaning is the only true stance from which any communication can occur — this authenticity constituting "the only life worth living." Although sexuality will continue to form a major part of his deliberations, the bottom line is not sexuality but death, the fact that sexuality buys the continuation of the species at the price of individual mortality. This is for Lacan the true, irrevocable, and "incurable" base of human alienation which must be made conscious and confronted.

> ...sexuality is represented in the psyche by a revelation of the subject that is deduced from something other than sexuality itself. ...the living being, by being subject to sex, has fallen under the blow of individual death."[3]

In fact, it is our fear of death, of separation, that is responsible for the construction and maintenance of those deceptive, self-defeating shells we call our ego. "The tomb is the first symbol of man's presence."[4]

Anything visible or spoken is brought into being by placing boundaries on its possibilities. The minute you draw a line on a blank sheet of paper you are defining a limit, but without this limit the object as a visible entity, a presence, is impossible. For Lacan, the human being confronts this limit which defines her/his being the moment the infant realizes the mother (or more precisely the mother's breast, an *object petit a*) as separate. The ego is unconsciously constructed as a defense mechanism against the fear of death, represented by absence. Here Lacan builds on Freud's conjecture in *Beyond the Pleasure Principle* that "If we are to take it as a truth that knows no exception that everything living dies for *internal* reasons — becomes inorganic once again — then we shall be compelled to say that *'the aim of all life is death'*...[5] Freud continues a few pages later by speculating in such a case "the ('ego-instincts') exercise pressure towards death and the (sexual instincts) towards a prolongation of life."[6]

This complicates Freud's earlier exposition of the ego as mediator between the human being and the world balancing the demands of id and superego — the version, generally held by American analysts, summarized by Calvin Hall in his *Primer of Freudian Psychology*:

> In the well-adjusted person the ego is the executive of the personality, controlling and governing the id and the superego and maintaining commerce with the external world in the interest of the total personality and its far-flung needs.[7]

The direct consequence of Lacan positioning himself in opposition to the American school on this issue is that the main objective of Lacanian analysis now becomes to break down rather than reinforce the ego. The ego is no longer "in the interest of the personality," it is the mechanism that keeps the true personality from emerging. The ego is the enemy.

The ego is the result of our fantasy that love can reunite us with what we have lost. Love grows out of desire, the yearning to no longer be separate, separated, from "the other." Plato's *Symposium* is, for Lacan, container of the prototypical myth of "love as unity" as well as the harbinger of the subversive underpinning of desire. In Plato's myth, the original sexes are pictured as three: male, representing the sun; female, representing the earth; and male/female, representing the moon, the combination of earth and sun. Because of their threat to the gods, they are each split in two, their original formation dictating their desire (the new male/male combination being the most "valiant" and "manly" and "when they grow up our statesmen.") It is from this state of affairs that love is born: "...human nature was originally one and we were a whole, and the desire and pursuit of the whole is called love."[8]

But even in Plato there is an indication that something is amiss:

> For the intense yearning which each of them has towards the other does not appear to be the desire of lover's intercourse, but of something else which the soul of either evidently desires and cannot tell, and of which she has only a dark and doubtful presentiment.[9]

If ego formation begins with desire, desire is born as the direct result of the infant's experience of the absence of the *object petit a*. We desire the mother, but more important, *we desire her to desire us* — desire being the direct consequence of the recognition of and necessity to eliminate lack. Only through the mother's desiring us will her presence be guaranteed to us, our satisfaction secured, and death/separation conquered. Here Lacan's scenario posits love as our fantasy barrier against death — the fantasy of re-union for which we become willing to sacrifice our own being in order to construct ourselves in the image of another's desire.

Enter the castration complex. Because of the intervention of the father as the "Name-of-the-Father" (*the law,* incest taboo) and because it is the father, the phallus, the mother desires, the mother becomes forbidden to us, and a cycle of displacement begins in which we are constantly searching for a replacement for our forbidden desire. We constantly search for fulfillment by building our ego in the image of another's desire. With the intervention of the "Name-of-the-Father" comes law, order, the syntax (order, law) of language. And the child, with language, names, becomes named, becomes subject (subjected, subjugated).

In the beginning is the Word:

> The psychoanalytic experience has rediscovered in man the imperative of the Word as the law that has formed him in its image.[10]

But the castration complex is many layered. On one hand, it is the confrontation of the child with the "Name-of-the-Father"; on another, it is the trauma of finding the mother castrated (lacking the phallus); in yet another, the trauma occurs when the child observes the sexual act between the parents with the disappearance and reappearance of the penis, implicitly making the mother herself the castrator.

Whatever the case, love is a fantasy which can never be realized, perpetuating itself in neurotic repetition and frustration, building ego image upon image, reflection upon reflection. Creating death of life.

The Self Divided

Not only is love (the union with an-other) an illusion, so is the unity of that entity calling itself by our proper name. This misrepresentation begins at the mirror stage as children "assume an image"[11] when, upon seeing their physical reflection in the mirror as a *gestalt,* a unit, they conceptualize themselves as "one."

It is interesting in this context to recount the conclusion of Hermann Hesse's *Steppenwolf*, which has an uncanny resemblance to Lacan's picture of the multiplicity of the self, especially if you substitute the figure of Lacan for the mysterious Pablo, and the "unconscious" for the soul.

The climax of *Steppenwolf* begins with the protagonist Harry Haller entering Pablo's Magic Theater. In the Dionysian revelry that follows, Haller's "personality (is) dissolved in the intoxication of the festivity like salt"[12] and he loses himself in a dance called "Yearning," only to be brought back to his senses by a look from his beloved Hermaine: "At this look that seemed to come from my own soul all reality fell away, even the reality of my sensuous love for her. Bewitched we looked at one another, while my poor little soul looked at me."[13]

At this moment Pablo appears with the message that Harry's longing for another reality must be found within himself. Pablo can only give him "the opportunity, the impulse, the key."[14] And so Harry relinquishes the mirror image of the material world, his body, unity, and looks into the mirror of the multiplicity of his soul. He chooses from among many alternatives that present themselves to him a dimly lit room in which a man who closely resembles Pablo is sitting in a posture of Eastern meditation before a huge chessboard on which the pieces of the soul, like chessmen, stand arrayed. This is a room, like the forest in *Through the Looking Glass*, in which there are no names. Harry is invited to offer up the pieces of his own broken personality with these words:

> The mistaken and unhappy notion that a man is an enduring unity is known to you. It is also known to you that man consists of a multitude of souls, of numerous selves...[15]

This, however, does not mean that our fate is completely out of our hands. To the contrary:

> It is wrong (to) hold that one only and binding and lifelong order is possible for the multiplicity of subordinate selves... We demonstrate to anyone whose soul has fallen to pieces that he can rearrange these pieces of a previous self in what order he pleases, and so attain to an endless multiplicity of moves in the game of life.[16]

As Harry himself finally realizes as the book ends and he confronts the "authenticity" of the game which is his existence:

I knew all the hundred thousand pieces of life's game were in my pocket. A glimpse of its meaning had stirred my reason and I was determined to begin the game afresh. I would sample its tortures once more and shudder again at its senselessness. I would traverse not once more, but often, the hell of my inner being.[17]

And the only course of action given the set of circumstances which is our lives:

One day I would be a better hand at the game. One day I would learn how to laugh...[18]

Woman as Object Subject to the Male

It is Hermaine's gaze that has brought Haller to his senses, but what about her? It is certainly more than coincidental that the names Hermaine and Harry are so close (as are the names Harry Haller and the author Hermann Hesse), no doubt suggesting that Hermaine is part and parcel of Hermann/Harry himself. There is no *separate* woman, human being, at all.

Woman is a symptom because as an individual living person she is perceived by the male only as part of his pathology. She is not another subject, a being apart from him; she has no existence apart from his fantasy solution of love and sexual reunion. Woman remains forever problematic because she symbolizes both the illusory original union and the lack, the gap, (perhaps even the "slit" of the unconscious) which is caused by the trauma of separation from her. Sexual or intimate relationships with women must therefore be analyzed in the same way a dream is, as a symptom, holding within its rebus the censored expressions of the unconscious. As Freud writes in *The Interpretation of Dreams*:

My patients...taught me that a dream can be...traced backwards in memory from a pathological idea. It was then only a short step to treating the dream itself as a symptom and to applying to dreams the method of interpretation that had been worked out for symptoms.[19]

While Lacan gives a particularly astute analysis of male pathology in a patriarchal society, he is no friend of women's liberation. On one hand he argues against Freud's concept of female masochism,

> But the supposed value, for example, of *feminine masochism*, as it is called, should be subjected, parenthetically, to serious scrutiny. It belongs to a dialogue that may be defined, in many respects, as a masculine phantasy. There is every reason to believe that to sustain this phantasy would be an act of complicity on our part.[20]

On the other, he can declare in his essay, "Aggressivity in Psychoanalysis," that the "barbarism of (this) the Darwinian century" is due to the "increasing absence of all those saturations of the superego and ego ideal that are realized in all kinds of organic forms in traditional societies, forms that extend from the rituals of everyday intimacy to the periodical festivals in which the community manifests itself." (Most of the traditional societies he refers to — ancient China and India being examples — were both sexist and hierarchical.)

> Furthermore, in abolishing the cosmic polarity of the male and female principles, our society undergoes all the psychological effects proper to the modern phenomenon known as the 'battle between the sexes' — a vast community of such effects, at the limit between the 'democratic' anarchy of the passions and their desperate leveling down by the 'great winged hornet' of narcissistic tyranny.[21]

Lacan does not listen to women. He dismisses the ideas of the women analysts who surround him, setting himself up as more feminist than they are — which might be true considering that in order to be heard by him they are probably encumbered by speaking out of the tradition he represents rather than their own experience as women. Or perhaps if women analysts and other women say nothing original to him about women's experience, it is not because they have nothing to say, but because they have nothing to say he wants or expects to hear. By the early 70s, when many of these remarks occur, there was a substantial body of work by women to relate to, even though important works like Adrienne Rich's *Of Woman Born* would come a few years later.

Moreover, any relationship of love apart from the sexual is ignored. Not only is the vagina considered a non-organ sexually, even the attributes that stereotypically accrue to it — gestation,

184

birth, nurturing — are left out altogether (as is true also of Freud.) Nurture is only seen from the child's point of view, when the child faces the possibility of losing the mother's sustenance. The perspective of the mother is of no account, except for the fact, for Lacan, that she desires the phallus over the child — a hypothesis that raises contradictions even in Freud, who at one point in *Civilization and Its Discontents* states that the original family was founded when "the male acquired a motive for keeping the female, or speaking more generally, his sexual objects near him: while the female, who did not want to be separated from her helpless young, was obliged, in their interests, to remain with the stronger male."[22]

It is not enough in this context to counter the phallus is more than the penis or sex, it represents power and that law which protects the mother. The mother in Freud's illustration *does not desire* the law, she *tolerates it* in order to protect her child.

Furthermore, as much as Lacan talks about the phallus being symbolic and not the organ, the penis, his theories about sexual dysfunction and perversion abound with what can only be called sexist assumptions based on physical anatomy — described at length in Benvenuto and Kennedy's *The Works of Jacques Lacan: An Introduction.*[23]

The last and most deadly generalization about women follows directly from Lacan's assumption that the principle of law, of order, of order*ing* is masculine. With language, the ability to name things and bring them into being as objects, (order them, put them into an order) comes the ability to name ourselves thereby *bringing ourselves into being* as subjects. Law here is seen as equivalent to order (ordering and giving orders) and is the province of the father (The Father), the patriarch (the Lord of the patriarchs). Without language, the ability to name ourselves, we *literally* lose consciousness. We cease to exist.

> In Lacan's view, the father introduces the principle of law, in particular the law of the language system. When this law breaks down, or if it has never been acquired, then the subject may suffer from psychosis.[24]

Woman is placed here outside language, outside the law. And this is precisely where the *unique* experience of the woman (when it happens, it is not by any means universal) is placed according to Lacan. He positions the woman as mystic, beyond the physical altogether, outside the mundane trivia of order in the everyday world — the traditional argument of the church fathers, even though Lacan disagrees with them about what mysticism entails. Lacan's own words:

> Today, however, my objective is to show you precisely in what he exists, this good old God. The mode in which he exists may well not please everyone, especially not the theologians who, as I have been saying for a long time, are far more capable than I am of doing without his existence. Unfortunately I am not quite in the same position because I am dealing with the Other. This Other, while it may be one alone, must have some relation to what appears of the other sex.[25]

The Other (capital O) can only refer to the unconscious: the other (small o), to woman. And here we come smack against that mystery, the Unconscious, the place beyond subject/object, good and evil. That mysterious entity/place, whatever it is: syntax in its most universal sense as law (read *order*), language, our censored history, the missing universal, the transcendent God. Perhaps all of these on different levels, or none of them, or more? The Unconscious is described in several essays by Lacan using very blatant female sexual imagery as the "gap," "slit," "pulsation."

But what concerns us most about Lacan is not the *Other*, it is what finally will be the fate of that other *other* — the human being called "woman" — not as saint, not even as mother, but *as a human being who has a right to demand a say over her own life.*

To summarize: when Lacan deals in his later essays directly with the demands of living women rather than that theoretical abstraction by which men define themselves, the feminine, he offers women only two alternatives, either the same fate as men, the same de-centered self, the same *angst*, including the castration complex in much the same way men experience it, or by "kicking her upstairs," implies that in her ability to be in contact with the Other, women are superior to men:

> There are men who are just as good as women. It does happen. And who therefore feel just as good. Despite, I won't say their phallus, despite what encumbers them on that score, they get the idea, they sense that

there must be a *jouissance* which goes beyond. That is what we call a mystic.[26]

It is very seductive, very traditionally seductive, to be spoken of in this way, but what does it really mean? Remember, for Lacan, language in every aspect, including ordinary language, is male. By accepting his premises women are doomed *by definition* to be forever without expression.

In the 70's, the poet Robert Creeley, a very sympathetic and charismatic figure, speaking on a panel at the University of Buffalo, voiced just such a notion — how men can only seek what women somehow are in touch with naturally, and, consequently, that is why men have to be, *are forced to be,* the writers, poets, politicians, and philosophers. Women don't need to and shouldn't involve themselves in such pedestrian occupations. Occupations which, unfortunately for us women, include the power to describe what we are and how we are to live in the world, that involve decisions vital to our lives. Creeley, who could here be Lacan himself, enunciates this eloquently in his poem, "The Name" as he writes to his daughter, counseling her:

Be natural
daughter, wise

as you can be,
all my daughters,
be women
for men

when that time comes.
Let the rhetoric
stay with me
your father. Let

me talk about it,
saving you such
vicious self-
exposure, let you

pass it on
in you. I cannot
be more than the man
who watches.[27]

Lacan. Not the man who watches, the one who listens. About women. To everyone one it seems, but women themselves.

The Subject Subjected

If Freud internalized Nietzsche's Dionysian primal force, Lacan carries that internalization one step further. Now the "other/Other" regardless of its status as person, personification, social relation becomes an internalized part of the individual whose unconscious somehow stands inside/outside her/himself. Everything becomes the subject, but not a subject in focus, a subject misted over, obscured, bound by an inner voice speaking a remote and difficult language. Only through analysis can we recognize ourselves, realize ourselves as part of this mystery, forever doomed to be split, fragmented, de-centered.

Created as subjects by language, we are chained to it, our identity contingent on its laws, its syntax. Without it we are literally no-thing, no-one, we do not exist.

Lacan uses the word "subject" here in the pejorative sense which is a difficult concept to grasp accustomed as we are by ordinary usage to thinking of the subject as active, in control, as opposed to the object which is passive, controlled. For Lacan, we are subject to, subjected by the restrictions of language, the law, our only path out through the doors of the saint or the madman. We must learn, like Harry Haller, to flow with and finally to laugh at our fate.

But, for Lacan, without the intervention of the analyst, without Pablo around to guide us, that is impossible. We are sent back again to the priesthood, to the necessity of an intermediary for knowledge. There is no way to explore the unconscious on our own except through making a subject/object of ourselves, thereby risking psychosis, becoming mad. As much as Lacan talks about equalizing the relationship between analyst and patient, it is the analyst who calls the shots, who determines the length of the session, who determines if what the patient is saying is "empty narrative," who gets paid. As Shoshanna Felman so succinctly puts it in *Jacques Lacan and the Adventure of Insight:*

It is by structurally occupying the position of the analysand's unconscious, and by thus making himself a student of the patient's knowledge, that the analyst becomes the patient's teacher — makes the patient learn *what would otherwise remain forever inaccessible to him.*[28]

Inaccessible, that is, unless we are privileged to somehow break free of this subject/object language which defines us, limits us, brings us into being, in some mystical, unspeakable freedom which can, only for a moment, be ours — like Saint Theresa on one hand, Zarathustra on the other. But that moment belongs to very few and even then it is limited. At best, for the rest of us the psychology of Lacan suffers from exactly the same dilemma known in Marxism as "economism," that somehow reaching this authentic "je" *I* (subject as free) as opposed to the imaginary "moi" me (subject as bound, as object) will *automatically* create some kind of mutual bond between people, even if based on mutual *angst*.

What Lacan is actually offering us is, according to John Rajchman in his article, "Lacan and the Ethics of Modernity," an amoral ethics, the notion of a de-centered but authentic sexuality based from a de-centered but authentic perspective of the world. Lacan in "Of the Subject of Certainty" makes the statement that "The status of the unconscious, which, as I have shown, is so fragile on the ontic plane, is ethical."[29] This statement combined with his conception of language, the law, and the unconscious leads to, in Rajchman's formulation, a theory of the subject that "can formulate no *morality*."[30]

> Thus Lacan reads Kant together with Sade, and not with Rousseau, as an anticipation of Freud. Lacan does not treat Sade as a case of sexual disorder. Rather he thinks that Sade formulated a modern ethic: one of law and transgression rather than of Harmonious nature, community, or the good life.[31]

There is a painting by the French Surrealist Rene Magritte which shows a man looking into a mirror, but instead of the mirror reflecting his face it reflects the back of his head. Perhaps the mirror Jacques Lacan holds up to us is of the same kind. Instead of showing us the originary point of our identity, it reflects instead our modern pathology, and can enlighten us neither about where we are going nor where we have been.

Partial Solutions

The age of technology is the age of the binary system — either A or not A, A or B. An electric current is either on or off. The classical world as described by Plato and later the Platonists is the world of the triad. Between night and day there is the twilight of dusk and dawn which is neither and partakes of both. Separating winter and summer are the inbetween seasons of spring and fall. Between the real world of forms and the unreal world of imagining there is the twilight world of multiples which partakes in the real world as a mirror reflects a real image in its depths.

Lacan, like Plato, deals with a tripartite universe in which one level refers to, represents, reflects the others. For Plato, the world of appearances, the visible world, is composed of two levels, one of tangible objects, multiple imitations or representations of the concepts of the real world and the other of imaginary constructions (like hallucinations, dreams and art) which imitate visual objects but are thrice removed from reality. For Lacan, the world of consciousness, of appearances, is also divided into two: the symbolic and the imaginary. For Lacan, like Plato, the real world is the world of true knowledge, causal, primary. For Lacan, like Plato, the visible world contains only images, representations — the higher, symbolic; the lowest, "image-ing," imagining.

In Plato's *Republic* the classes are three: representing wisdom, the spirited element, the passions. Even the original sexes are three. In Lacan the symbolic "Name-of-The-Father" is also a play on the traditional Christian triad (three in one): "In the Name of The Father, The Son, and The Holy Ghost." The primal psychic trauma takes place in the triad of mother, father, child. The therapeutic situation — the only one in which the Other (the unconscious) can be heard because it is the other (the analyst) who can hear it — is triadic, consisting of the patient, the patient's unconscious, the analyst.

Analysis progresses through the speech of the subject in so far as it passes *beyond the dual relation*, and thus no longer encounters anything except the absolute Other, whom the subject doesn't know how to recognize."[32]

In Lacan, as in many of his contemporaries, structure becomes meaning. The signifier refers not to an object or definition (the signifier "chair" referring to the object "chair"), but to another signifier. It is the grammar of the sentence, the relationship of one word to another, not the definition of the words within the sentence that hold meaning. Meaning is an inventory, like rifling through a desk drawer, the significance of which is contained in the series of items it accommodates. In his later lectures Lacan comes to concentrate more and more on mathematical models of "chains of signifiers" to illustrate his concepts. Instead of diagraming complex sentences, he diagrams the complexity of differing relationships, these models not to be worked out algebraically, but to stand as graphic representations of the linking that analysis explores. They are a logical calculus of the psyche, a different kind of logic, but no less pernicious or constraining than traditional logic.

The contradictions of the Industrial Revolution if anything have been exacerbated by the switch to electronic technology. Television, radio and film may have brought the world into the living room, but in many instances they have taken our person out of the world. Jacques Lacan rails against repetition, imitation, the "one-dimensional man," the clone. But the dilemma of the Electronic Age remains alienation as much if not more than conformity, because it is alienation and that by-product of alienation, despair, with its resultant self-insolation that makes the rest of our problems of racism, sexism, economic injustice, homophobia, even problems of intimacy, impossible to solve. And it is difficult to see how Lacan's psychology speaks to the problem of isolation and alienation, beyond positing it as the universal human condition.

The critical word here is "change." Many political activists, particularly since the women's movement, have now realized the *necessity* of taking the personal into consideration. Consciousness-raising, one of our most important tools, is a direct product of Freud's insight into the internalization of social paradigms. It is now time for more psychoanalysts to integrate a progressive world view into their theory and teaching, and into their practice. Those analysts who continue to divorce themselves from personal responsibility for social problems, who continue, like Lacan (and Freud before him), to consider altruism an aberration, who continue to exclude the point of view of women along with anyone else who happens to fall outside traditional Western exegesis, who persist in mirroring rather than dealing with oppressive systems will inevitably be trapped in their own solipsistic universe and remain part of the problem, rather than part of the solution.

That is why the real future of psychoanalysis, if it is to have one, lies not with Lacan and his followers but with those who, like Frantz Fanon, realize value judgements are inevitable, history is fraught with meaning. It belongs to those who understand that what forms the pathology of individuals depends finally not only on an understanding of their past, both familial and social, but on their relationship to their present and to the future. Both society's and their own.

NOTES

1. Jacques Lacan, *The Four Fundamental Concepts of PsychoAnalysis*, p.20.
2. Jacques Lacan, *Écrits*, p.50.
3. Jacques Lacan, *The Four Fundamental Concepts of Psycho-Analysis*, p.204-205.
4. John P. Muller and William J. Richardson, *Lacan and Language*, p.107.
5. Sigmund Freud, *Beyond the Pleasure Principle*, p.32. (Italics author's.)
6. *Ibid.* p.38.
7. Calvin S. Hall, *A Primer of Freudian Psychology*, p.28.
8. Plato, *Selected Dialogues*, p.326.
9. *Ibid.*
10. Jacques Lacan, *Écrits*, p.106.
11. Jacques Lacan, *Écrits*, p.2.
12. Hermann Hesse, *Steppenwolf*, p.193.

13. *Ibid* p.197.
14. *Ibid* p.201.
15. *Ibid* p.218-219.
16. *Ibid*
17. *Ibid* p.248.
18. *Ibid*
19. Sigmund Freud, *The Interpretation of Dreams*, p.133.
20. Jacques Lacan, *The Four Fundamental Concepts of Psycho-Analysis*, p.192.
21. Jacques Lacan, *Écrits*, p.26-27.
22. Sigmund Freud, *Civilization and Its Discontents*, p.46.
23. Bice Benvenuto and Roger Kennedy, *The Works of Jacques Lacan*, pp.132-141.
24. *Ibid* p.131.
25 Jacques Lacan, *Feminine Sexuality*, p.141.
26. *Ibid* p.147.
27. Robert Creeley, *For Love*, pp.144-145.
28. Shoshanna Felman, *Jacques Lacan and the Adventure of Insight*, p.83. Italics mine.
29. Jacques Lacan, *The Four Fundamental Concepts of Psycho-Analysis*, p.33.
30. John Rajchman, "Lacan and the Ethics of Modernity," p.43.
31. *Ibid* p.50.
32. Jacques Lacan, *The Seminar of Jacques Lacan: Book II*, p.270. Italics mine.

BIBLIOGRAPHY

Benvenuto, Bice and Kennedy, Roger. *The Works of Jacques Lacan*. New York: St. Martin's Press. 1986.

Creeley, Robert. *Poems 1950-1960*. New York: Charles Scribner's Sons. 1962

Fanon, Frantz. *The Wretched of the Earth*. New York: Grove Press. 1963.

Felman, Shoshana. *Jacques Lacan and the Adventure of Insight*. Cambridge, London: Harvard University Press. 1987.

Freud, Sigmund. *Beyond the Pleasure Principle*. Translated and edited by James Strachey. New York, London: W.W.Norton & Company. 1961.

—. *Civilization and Its Discontents*. The Standard Edition translated by James Strachey. New York, London: W.W.Norton & Company. 1961.

—. *The Interpretation of Dreams*. Translated from the German and edited by James Strachey. New York: Avon Books. 1965.

Hall, Calvin S. *A Primer of Freudian Psychology*. (A Mentor Book.) New York: New American Library. 1979.

Hesse, Hermann. *Steppenwolf*. Translated by Basil Creighton. New York: Bantam Books. 1929.

Lacan, Jacques. *Écrits*. New York, London: W.W.Norton & Company. 1977.

—. *The Four Fundamental Concepts of Psycho-Analysis*. Edited by Jacques-Alain Miller. Translated from the French by Alan Sheridan. New York, London: W.W.Norton & Company. 1973.

—. *The Seminar of Jacques Lacan*. Book I, Freud's Papers on Technique 1953-1954. Edited by Jacques-Alain Miller. Translated with notes by John Forrester. New York, London: W.W.Norton & Company. 1988.

—. *The Seminar of Jacques Lacan*. Book II, The Ego in Freud's Theory and in the Technique of Psychoanalysis 1954-1955. Edited by Jacques-Alain Miller. Translated by Sylvana Tomaselli. With notes by John Forrester. New York, London: W.W.Norton & Company. 1988.

Lacan, Jacques and the *école freudienne*. *Feminine Sexuality*. Edited by Juliette Mitchell and Jacqueline Rose. Translated by Jacqueline Rose. New York, London: W.W.Norton & Company. 1983.

Muller, John P. and Richardson, William J. *Lacan and Language*. New York: International Universities Press, Inc. 1982.

Plato. *Selected Dialogues*. Translated by Benjamin Jowett. Pennsylvania: The Franklin Library. 1983.

—. *The Republic*. Translated and with introduction and notes by Francis MacDonald Cornford. London, Oxford, New York: The Oxford University Press. 1941.

Rajchman, John. "Lacan and the Ethics of Modernity." Representations 15, University of California Press, Summer 1986.

Turkle, Sherry. *Psychoanalytic Politics*. New York: Basic Books, Inc. 1978.

Creativity & Change

if you were to ask me what defines me
how I place myself in the world
I would say this poem
is the center of it   is the core
that I reach toward the world
as I reach toward you
as one who wants to reach out
endlessly   who wants to open out
endlessly   who wants to feel
endlessly   that question
that is our lives

One describes motion not only by the arms, the legs, the body that
does the moving, but by the space around each form that allows motion to
exist at all. As motion is process, perhaps the most basic of all, so also
"creativity" and "change" are words of process, words of relationship. Art
is to creativity as a person's arms are to their motion, a tangible means of
action. As not only one part, but the entire human form moves through
space.

The creative process is dependent on a recognition of relationship,
usually between two objects not normally related. As all things are
irrelevant until needed and form the background of our lives. As a child
is born or an idea. Or as a need emerges and is seized.

To talk about contradiction is to talk about conflict. It is to talk
about the relationship of separate parts to each other and to the whole.
To talk about unity is to talk about synthesis. It is to talk about the
whole in relationship to its parts. As it is through our words, the
structure of our thoughts, that the world forms itself around us and we
focus ourselves in it. To speak of form without content or content without
form is to speak on one side of death and on the other of chaos.

Marx stated that the primary function of philosophy is not to record
history, but to change history. Creativity is the process by which one
changes the world. Not through "steady, inevitable change," but as an act
of transformation, of magic. Not the magic of the supernatural, separated from the human being, but the magic of human beings themselves.

The series of events in an individual's or a community's life are not
haphazard. Beneath every action there is a guiding idea which links it
to every other action. At the base of every idea there is a history of
actual events.

197

The Nineteenth Century, the century of Darwin, of mechanism, held a concept of change which, although cruel, was detached, objective, steady, and seemingly entirely predictable. The Twentieth Century is a time characterized by violent, cataclysmic change — a time in which everything has been brought into question, in which the laws of nature themselves hold only according to a particular context, a time in which there seems to be no central guiding principle, except perhaps that to be found in the principle of change itself.

In the 1950s, brought on perhaps more than anything else by the total dislocation of the Second World War, with the first tide of the dispossessed, the Beat Generation, came the beginning of the cultural rebellion in the United States and its single most important consequence — that people began to think about culture as something that was an expression of the way they lived, rather than something they did on weekends or in the evening to relax or that they went to the university to get a Ph.D in. That culture is an expression of the life of a community of people, the same way a poem or painting is an expression of a person's life, an experience, a synthesis of thought and feeling. An action.

Culture is more than "art." It is inseparable from the larger community of human beings of which it is a part. The human being becomes once more the center of the universe, the place from which all things begin. It is people that revolution, that change is about, as creativity, as art, is always about people, is always created from the heart and mind and dreams of the human being. It is the human form, the human dream that becomes the center of focus. It is human energy that guides the dream.

The art of the future is art which reflects this change and art which, by its nature, produces even greater change.

Forces outside of us make and mold us, as we shape them, also, to fit our own needs. No book is written in a vacuum, no idea is born from a void. Space is filled with people and ideas, with nameless form, with content. The question then is how to hold these ideas, how to form them, see their relations. How to understand that process of which we are only a part.

FREEING THE BALANCE

In contemporary times, there has been a radical shift of emphasis from things, objects, people to the background, "field," the context that makes things possible — the silences that shape words, the relationships that define people, the needs that focus our attention on each other, on our world. Consequently, there has been a shift from description and analysis of "things" to an attempt to understand activity, function, process, "work." The background ceases to be the static painted flats of the theater, and becomes a set of relationships, of inter-relationships, of needs. The line of contact is not unidirectional, radiating out from one isolated center. It is a dialogue. We become, in a literal sense, not actors on an empty stage, but activities in silence, formed and focused, brought into speech, by our interaction with each other.

The danger is with this shift in emphasis the individual (whether person or thing) can be misplaced. It is all too easy when making a generalization about relationship to exclude those making the relationship possible. And with this removal of structure from content, the fullness, richness, the uniqueness of each individual and each relationship is lost. By subsuming everything under the abstract activity, the mathematical or logical relationship, we have the tendency to lose the tangibleness, the substantiality, and sometimes even the fact of existence. This is particularly important to recognize now in view of our increasing dependence on electronic technology and computers, graphs and statistics. Even though pointed in a different direction, we are still imprisoned by old prejudices, old habits of thinking, old methods, old speech patterns, old rules. We are still bound by a system of logic that abstracts form from content whether that content be person, object or action, that refuses to recognize the multi-leveled nature of reality, that condemns us to choosing between partial truths. That keeps us powerless.

What is needed are not new words or new definitions, but a radical shift in our way of looking at our world. Any resolution to a problem brought about in the first place by the oppressiveness of the society in which we move is not going to be found using that society's logic. In fact, it is precisely this conditioning — a conditioning that denies any system as "unreal" that does not fit within the traditional intellectual framework — that holds us back. It is not really true that "seeing is believing." We can see things and still not believe them if they do not fit into our preconceived notion of how things should be.

As social beings, our primary commitment is to the group; as artists, to the vision, the work. At its two extremes this dichotomy is seen as the conflict between "art as propaganda" and "art for art's sake." The former is a totally utilitarian view of art; the latter (the most accepted and acceptable critical view in the U.S. at the present time) is that the purpose of art, if it has any, is found in its own self-identity, in a self-contained realm cut off from the rest of experience.

But the aesthetic experience is not something separate from the rest of our lives. The poem, if allowed to sing freely through us, can teach us how to reach beyond imposed limitations — as can any free action or thought which manages somehow to escape the rigid self-censorship we impose on each other and on our world. This, however, is not to suggest that technique is not necessary or that we have no social responsibility. It is only through skill (an entirely different concept than manipulation) and responsibility (not to be confused with control) that this type of freedom is possible. In order to sing you must have a voice, and it is precisely through discipline and a consciousness of our relationship to others that we find our voice.

Usually when we think of the word "balance," we think of equalization, of symmetry — if one side of the scale is too heavy, you move the weighting mechanism until the two "balance." The artist is seen as walking a tightrope between vision and necessity, art and life. But there is another way of looking at this word. In the earliest Tarot decks the first card, "The Juggler," balances the four elements which represent the universe. In that same way I, as an artist, hold in suspension different and seemingly contradictory elements of the outside world and my own life, thoughts, objects, actions. Through the creative process, I focus these elements and discover their relationships. This is done through that central unifying experience which is the work of art.

The model of the scale is a mechanical model — the human being is needed only to place and move. The model of the juggler, however, is an organic model. The elements are not "two," but as many as skill allows. The human being is central, a living element who "balances" the rest. And with this shifting of understanding, our sense of time shifts. We no longer think in terms of a series of points in logical sequence, but of association, relationship, context, change.

Art embraces contradiction. It is not possible to talk about a poem or a painting, sculpture, musical composition as if it were an object. Neither is it a process. Poetry is as much a multiplicity and a single unit, a completed moment (an object) and an action (a process) as the poet, the human being behind the poem. The individual poem might alter relative to place and time, but there always remains that thread which weaves through individual works and sings the poem as name.

The work of art is, as a person is, both memory (the past) and activity (the present). It is, as each human being is, at each moment *simultaneously* complete and in the process of completion. However, unlike the poet, whose existence as a living being is constant, the poem is actualized only upon being written or read. As the poet finishes the poem, readers seize and interpret it, live it, according to their own individual experiences and needs. At its best, the poem, any art work, is multi-leveled, holding many levels of meaning without sacrificing any — the most mundane or the most profound.

The concepts *balance* and *completion* must be understood not as the median between two extremes, as the "end" of a logical process, but as the organic suspension and assimilation of elements of experience. The way I wrote and what I wrote when I was twenty differ from the subject matter and style I write in today. With years come changes; yet, at twenty, I wrote poems that continue to grow in meaning for me.

Because of the prejudices of our modern world, we are forced literally to live "by the clock." One moment follows the next. One heartbeat succeeds another. We are imprisoned in an endless one-directional sequence of action. The question, "Why?" (the basis of all meaning) is labeled "nonsense" and replaced by the question, "How?" An examination of sequential process, cause and effect, takes the place of a quest for understanding until everything is reduced to an analysis of method, and we find ourselves walking backward, measuring our lives by our footprints.

The question is not "art for art's sake" versus "political art." In fact, the discoveries of the work of art cannot exist without the understanding of relationship that is an integral part of social interaction. However, at the same time every work of art expresses a set of social relationships and gives information about our social position and biases, there is also a part of the work that exists apart from us, from our personal or social needs, demands, control. It is precisely this most precious part of the work, the part that we "let be," that reveals what is new to us, makes our world ever new to us.

Whatever new contradictions, whatever new theories evolve, the essential questions can never be asked, much less resolved, unless they risk real pain, unless they bring something new into being. Unless they have the capacity to transmute, to transform, to change.

If there is one thing poetry, both others and my own, has shown me, it is the error of approaching the world as an "expert" declaring, "I know what you are. My search is how to make you work for me." But rather, to approach the world in ever renewed wonder, with a request: "I thought I knew you, but you are more than I ever thought possible. Teach me how to be."

New York, 1981

DEFINITIONS

1.
I think it's coming close to death
that does it
          both others
     & your own
that magnifies the values
begins the definitions

This morning
          mild at last
     after weeks of chill
Streets heavy with water
People stepping
               cautiously
     hardly knowing where
     to place their feet
so accustomed to barriers
                    of salt and ice

My mind resembles those winter streets
grey
     with sludge
The snow cover melted
The sidewalks washed of unfamiliar
glare

2.
After all   she said
What difference does it make?
That's the reason I never write
hardly speak   of what is me

I begin to answer glibly   stop
Held myself in identical fear
My own touch tentative
                    almost an excuse
like making love to someone

for the first time
or the third   (which is always harder)
once you begin to know   experience
another

    the tension of your hair   brown
    streaked with grey
    the lines of
    your face   like wires   rushing through
    my hands   the pressures of your past
    your forehead   your knees

3.
Warm outside   the steam
continues   forced by habit
I open the window   throw the
oracle   trace the heat
The heart thinks constantly it says
One constant then   the heart   another
the drawing back
        Four o'clock
two hours till dawn   Nightmare
image   your face
surrounded by strangers
Beloved   you turn   away

Sweat mixes with flowered sheets
The constant fear
           To push out
finally   cautiously   tentatively
and find

       an empty place

4.
Death brings us close to it
Death itself
      forgetting
And we the living
wanting to remember

not wishing to be forgotten
                    separated
from what we hold most near

I hold you for a moment   lose you
watch you disappear
                    I hold you
for a lifetime   lose you

the next year   the next morning
the next minute   the next breath

5.
You tell me
What can I say to that
young woman   18 years
of age?

That I at 38 must once more lay aside
all sense of definition   order
Must once more carefully measure
the accumulation of my years

Or should I say
her question can be answered
in specific needs   others
and her own
          But she's asking
more than that   We both know
what she means

The only real difference being death
The one who stops the heart

BARCELONA JOURNAL

I.

The hill is on fire. Orange rims it like the sun. It is such a clear day you can see the city in all directions. Houses poured into hills, until the hills themselves are really no more than waves of houses, frozen in cement, tile & brick — the color of muted earth. Ten miles away the hill is on fire & you can begin, even here, to smell smoke on the wind. People arrive with binoculars, telescopes. I have not seen it so clear for days. Buildings curve round into the sea. A border of dirt & sea. But now all eyes are directed toward the mountain. The crescent of orange fire barely visible through the smoke. The sun burns into my back. The other fire. That Spanish flame.

II.

Alien. There is no other word for it. For the first time, today, travelling this country road outside Barcelona, I realize I am away, far away, from home. All cities are in some respects the same. But here among grass and trees and hills and that strange mountain range, I feel the difference. Not as being estranged, divorced from, but as something stronger, something alien. Something unlike anything I have ever experienced before.

III.

These sudden rains. Not tropical — with lightning, thunder, great release after hours of tension. But more nonchalant, more "by-the-by." As if the clouds, rushing to get somewhere else, were to drop some rain in passing. And so it goes all day. First dark, then light, then dark, then light. A spotted day. Cool, but even a slow walk will bring perspiration. It is warm. No, that's not the word for it. Not cool, not warm. Tepid. The day is tepid. & slides by.

IV

PORTRAIT OF BOY, MAN & HORSE

How would they feel
if they knew they formed the subject
of this portrait?
Their only color the color
the boy's banging makes
against a large tin plate
What are they selling?
The odd shapes lining three sides
of a wooden crate tell nothing
hold their secret tight as glass
(sea-aged)
   The kind I held yesterday
at the shore
They remind me somehow of the sea
All motion and sound
On the surface thick
    almost monotonous
covering subtler shades
& deeper tones

V.

Time. I think on the way to the park of time. Of how, at the same
instant, I feel both the extension and the lack of it. As if there
were a moment, somewhere, hidden, that if touched would open
the heart of the world to me. And then, turning my head, I see the
hills, so green, so full, they seem without time, without extension.
Even the broken bottle in front of me is part of it. A piece of
mirror: a small black ant. A breeze so gentle it is almost
indistinguishable from the movement of children racing by. An
edge of clouds. And the sun. The sun! It's very heat forcing me
finally to turn away.

VI.

Am I, at last, learning to let things be? To sit & be in this place without fantasy or thought (the wish to be somewhere else, in another place). I recognize this as something very dear, very precious. When I move, must I lose it? Must even this perception remain in its own place? Can I carry it with me? Can I become it? Oh, if only I could become it. If only I could turn myself into this space.

VII.

JARDINERIA Y CONSTRUCCIONES MITJANS, S.A.

So it says on the side of the giant van
parked by two vehicles, the kind you use to
    flatten roads —
deserted —   it being 3 o'clock
    the workmen out to lunch —
2 small boys have taken over —
    dressed identically in blue-stripped
        shirts —
They tug at levers, shout
    commands neither I nor
        the machine understand —
& in their minds a road is built,
    a city, an empire
until their father arrives, short, stout
        & angry
like a brisk north wind,
    & chases them away —

VIII.

It is too hard to explain yourself to other people. Too tiring. I imagine long speeches. Never delivered. Or if begun, much less interesting to the person of flesh than to the creatures of my imagination. I speak of New York, a topic which never much interested me before, as if the city and I were one. As if by explaining how I live, where I eat, go to dance, have fun, what kind of friends I have, I explain myself. It is not the city, but me I want them to know. But I can never show them how I receive this world, what kind of person I really am, except, perhaps, by chance — with a touch, or a poem.

IX.

The real proof of what a person is like is how they act toward you when you are somehow at their mercy. How parents act with their children: how lovers act & friends. The measure being what is at stake. The test of a person — how they use power. How they abuse or refuse control.

X.

How small everything is. This old villa, only three hundred years ago, a dwelling place. People lived here, moved around these rooms from day to day, doing things people did then (and now). But the wax figures of these people, the old man bent over his desk, the mother with her candlesticks, the soldier writing orders, are so small. And their clothing, thick, hand-sewn, is awkward, graceless. I can't get used to this house, or these people. I try to place myself back — what it must have been like. But size stops me, not time. This one small woman, no more than shoulder height, clothed in grey and blue, her hand resting gently on a table, looking silently into space.

XI.

The picture of Franco on the coins is gradually being replaced. A main thoroughfare no longer "Generalisimo Franco" (as on all the maps) is now called simply "Diagonal." It is hard for me to imagine what it must have been like here five years ago. Politics seems so far from me in this place. It waits for me at home, in my own language. If you can ever really leave it. The decisions. The implications. But here, now, for me, in the summer air, at least this one afternoon, an interval. A break.

XII.

There are no rules for it. I must learn how to move. I, who having moved too much, have never really learned to leave. A fish moves from tail to fin across great currents guided only by the way the water feels, its weight. But I cannot escape even one moment from myself. I bring all of it with me. Another day. In a different place. I glide by for two months, an instant. I do not even, as others, give the illusion of being here. Where am I then? If not here? Oh, Barcelona, how much you bring me home.

Barcelona, 1976

ANOTHER DAY

My stomach betrays me, she thought. I feel less than a minute, she smiled. A word sets it off, a phrase orders it, positions my mind like a railway conductor waving trains by, this one here, this one there. Hectic New York stations, full of cigarette butts and crushed papers, anonymous graffiti in garish colors, describing letters but never names; symbols, but never people.

It *is* a dull evening, she thought, and moved toward the window. One gets frantic seeing time pass, how quickly it passes; but even so, one must admit most evenings are dull. Sometimes they can be filled with a good book, an interesting movie, and even, on occasion, but rarer now (the best time being morning) with work. And sometimes people fill in the spaces. But often people make you feel even more empty, closing the air around them, letting you in only momentarily — the way one breathes in, recognizes, a strange but not unpleasant odor; in order to make a comment, change a mood.

In the afternoon you can walk; fine, long walks. Letting your body move, move! She laughed, remembering what a friend had said, was it really almost twenty years ago? Don't worry, she had said, no matter what you do, no matter what is done to you, at one precise moment, a moment which can be calculated years in advance, the sun comes up.

What *was* that noise outside? Was it that old man again singing in the street, cursing in his thick, rich accent? Soon windows would slam. Shouts would echo back and forth like shots across the street, cutting him down in their cross-fire. But wounded, bleeding, oblivious, he would continue on, singing and cursing his invisible demon, his creature, the world. Is it so strange, she thought, is he so crazy, don't we all of us do the same? All lines, fire aimed somehow at us, or missing us, but related somehow, here — she touched her heart, laughing again, quietly, at the thought. She pulled her chair over to the window, sat down looking out into the street.

Yes, there he is. Not so old really. Not if you looked closely enough. Maybe fifty-five, sixty. His hair not white at all, jet-black (what there was of it), pulled over his head like a tight, cheap cap. His face taut. Everything about him strained. As if he had stretched himself two inches above his normal height to more adequately meet his imagined world. Yes, there he is, silent now for a minute; thinking, building, planning his next move. Yes, he thinks too. We both do, she thought, and shook her head at the incongruity of it, at the inconsistency of it. We build our worlds in silence, he and I.

She smiled this time, but did not laugh. The thought wide enough for a smile, but not enough for laughter. Wide enough for a change of expression, a movement of the face, but not a vocalization, a sound. It was warm. A pleasant enough night, even if dull. I want to own things, she thought. I have an obsession to own things. To make sure they are there for me. She turned away from the window a moment, paused.

To think things dull is to believe you have nothing left to learn, to believe you know everything, have seen everything, have experienced everything. But how absurd, she thought, but nonetheless, she thought, sometimes I do get tired. Maybe that is how death takes us, disguised, poised to hold us when we need comfort and there is no one else around.

The day's routine had not been bad. The average number of successes and disappointments. It was primarily her stomach that betrayed her. Like a spider reaching for a hand-hold on the wall, sticking on, driven on, with a life and mind of its own. But no, not there! People are not walls. No place to weave your net, spin your delicate strands, your transparent web. And how it screamed as it fell; how it screamed as it died. The lifeline tossing it from the living wall.

No matter how I sit back, like now, tranquil, regarding it all with a thought, a smile, my body knows. My body feels around me, throws out its web, and sometimes is tossed back, and sometimes falls, and I can feel its scream, must live through the torture of its scream. She turned from the window, suddenly sad, suddenly in pain.

What time *is* it? How many hours until dawn? To get through this evening. Now no longer dull, but sharp and burning. Remember all evenings are not like this; tomorrow might be different. He might call or she might call or a letter come. But in the future, she thought, and thought, and thought, how many more evenings like this will there be? How many more evenings must I get through like this one?

Perhaps none. She froze. Perhaps this evening is the last. Terror struck her. Sometimes people leave you and you try so hard to see them again, at least one more time. But it is too late; they are gone. Maybe this evening is like that. A lover going away for the last time, escaping under a hood of darkness, of dullness, of burning — without warning, without words.

But I would welcome you back, she thought. Her eyes full now. I would welcome you back. Oh, please, come back! Whatever your disguise.

THE DEATH OF A FRIEND

Finally, perhaps, it is an accumulation of small things that changes us, the unexpected and sometimes almost unnoticed incidents that signal moments of transition, pointing us in an entirely different direction, almost without our knowledge, often without our consent.

November 17, 1963. A day I remember in sequences like an old-fashioned tableau, the players standing in different attitudes and poses, frozen. If I were to sum up that day now, thirteen years later, I would have to say that Alison was a victim of a conspiracy of "cooperation," — the illusion of protection, of being safe, of being taken care of, cared for, of having someone to lean on, someone to trust. It was a conspiracy, a betrayal, so old, so overused, so cliched she should have seen it. But she didn't. She couldn't afford to. And being faced with a reality so terrible she could not accept it, she simply refused to believe.

Nine o'clock. Fourteenth street. Rush hour. Cold. Windy. The bus is crowded. An old woman, pale, sits across the aisle from me, years hanging from her hands. I look out at the street between elbows and knees. A man coughs, lunges forward. No one moves. No one *can* move. There is a tinny sound in my ears, my mouth tastes funny. I feel tired, confused, a little sick. But it is bright out. The streets, what I can see of them, look clean and clear. It is hard to be worried on a morning like this. I look at Alison. She smiles, laughs, takes my hand.

Noon. We are still waiting, have been waiting for hours. In this basement, poor, cramped. How much all institutional rooms have in common. How easily one could be substituted for another. We could be almost anywhere — a criminal courtroom, a Medicaid Office, Welfare, the Unemployment Office, a hospital ward, a schoolroom in the Bronx or Brooklyn or Queens, Family Court. All painted in green. Serviceable green. Soothing green. Ugly, dull and boring green. Depressing green. Designed to keep you quiet, hypnotize you, make you incapable of thought, motion or speech.

A guard brings us coffee.

"Do you have a lawyer?"

"No."

"That's good."

"Good?"

"Sure."

"Why? I don't understand. I was thinking of asking for a postponement until I could get a lawyer."

"Look, this judge is a nice guy. He'll feel more sympathetic toward you if you go in there and sort of look to him for protection. He's very protective of mothers. A lawyer would just put him off." Helpful. Solicitous. "You're much better off this way, believe me. I've been here for fifteen years now. I know. This man doesn't believe children should be separated from their mother. He'll never take the kids away from you unless he gets mad for some reason. That's why it's better to appeal to him." He nudges her arm. "You know what I mean."

Turning to me. "Who are you?"

"I'm her friend. I came to testify for her."

"Do you want some more coffee? It could be a long time."

"Yes, some more coffee. Please."

Trust is, for some people, an automatic response. It is not in their nature to be suspicious of people. This was a trait Alison and I shared. It had been two years now since we met. We had been friends for one year, lovers for six months, and for the last six months I had hardly seen her. I had gotten tired of rats and footsteps on the roof, of obscene phone calls and staying up all night protecting a cat I had gotten to protect me, and had moved. But I came back on a distress call from Alison telling me her parents were threatening to take her children away from her and she had to go to court and would I come.

"But how could you possibly think that by swallowing paint it would come out of your fingertips and you could avoid using a brush?"

"It was a beautiful idea, wasn't it? I wanted to be close to the canvas, to touch it, to feel the color pouring out of me. I wanted to paint the sun."

The ceiling swayed back and forth. The floor tilted, folded, rocking gently like a ship. I grabbed for a chair, anything to hold me steady. I clutched the door frame. "Why didn't you tell me it was so strong?" Colors shot from the walls. Straight and sharp. So thick you could hold on to them. I was drifting in time. I stepped through the second hand of the old clock on the kitchen wall and everything stopped. The only sound was a faint, monotonous hum. Gold showered from the walls. It's just like Baudelaire, I thought, and laughed. The radio sounded like Donald Duck. Stop, I directed with my finger. And it stopped. Everything became perfectly motionless. Everything that was "real." I rose into the silence, my head inches from the ceiling. Alison swore she saw me disappear.

It was hours later when we first touched. We didn't even mean to. It certainly wasn't planned. We were exhausted and lay down, together, to sleep. And there it was between us, thick and impenetrable. I felt it shooting up and down my body. A feeling dense as fear.

Two o'clock. Four cups of coffee. The same room. Endless cigarettes. Should she call a lawyer, postpone the case? Could it even *be* postponed?

"What could they have against me? What did I do? What *should* I do?"

"Look, it can't hurt to postpone it. Get some better advice. Get more people together."

"But I want it over with. And maybe this guy is right. He seems nice enough and he should know. You heard what he said — they never take children from their mother. How much longer will it take? How much longer will they make us wait?"

"Alison. Listen."

"Look, it's all right. My parents are a little crazy. They want to worry me, keep me in line, make me like them. They object to my being a painter, a man I lived with they didn't like. They're only trying to scare me. They've been after me for years. But basically they love me. They wouldn't do anything to really hurt me."

"Alison..."

"Don't worry. I'm not worried. Everything will be all right. I'll just tell the judge how much I love my kids, what a good mother I am. You'll tell him." Smiling. "How could anyone not believe you, not trust you to tell the truth. Don't worry. I'll cooperate. I'll do anything they say. Everything will be fine."

They said she might have won finally, maybe even at the next hearing, if (on being told her children would be "temporarily" taken away) she hadn't hit the judge. I was never called. It was a set-up, a foregone conclusion, a trap. It was that particular form of punishment devised for those who create, who give birth.

After that Alison was never the same. She left Bellevue one week later only to be picked up again within the month, dragged screaming off the street by the police. Her parents came to collect her things. Her children were living with them, going to a private school in Colorado, learning the proper way to behave. There is one painting of hers I still have. A painting of the sun. An orange sun, its rays thick and impenetrable, sharp and straight.

BEGINNINGS

1.

When you hide, they search for you. Nothing must be missing. Everything must be in its correct, its proper place.

What does it take to change things? Does anyone or anything ever really change? Perhaps first of all one must consciously make a decision to allow change to enter. To become open to it. To sacrifice control. To break convention. To become someone new, someone different. To make a conscious decision to enter the unknown.

And sometimes you are thrown into it. Enter it almost by accident — the ultimate consequences being vague, obscure. As I entered Berkeley in 1959, New York in 1961. As I decided to go to Cuba that year, 1967, to return to New York, to a place I had lived for six years and see it for the first time. To become ill and experience pain. To live through, see through, months and months of pain.

Some things are not absurd, are not in themselves absurd. The Fool chases a butterfly. A dog snaps at his heels. In some worlds he is dressed in rags, in others in colors of yellow and red and green. In some worlds the Fool is a man. In others, a woman. In some places a child. In others, an adult. It is always a question of place. In another world it might be different. And, for moments, in this...

When did things begin to change for me? At what moment, in what year? When was it I began to feel a difference? It came in stages. First a sense of one thing, and then another. As a baby first grows and discovers, puts together, a world.

2.

If you ask for nothing, that is exactly what you get. Even if, on the other hand, you lay out your demands, your heart, inch by inch, anxious for negotiation, ready for compromise, the result is often the same. But at least something is spared.

If she were an umbrella, what kind of weather would she conceal? If she were a road, where would she wind? If she were a color, would she be bright or dull? How many miles would you have to walk her before you would begin to understand? How many times would you have to play her before you would begin to hear?

As a child, I closed the world around me like the pages of an unwanted book. I created another world, a world of dreams and pictures. I never confused the two worlds, never tried to mix them. The other, the world in which I could live, was always just around the corner, behind some secret door, hidden, but expected.

What does it mean to live with someone for six years and no longer remember the sound of their voice, what they ate for dinner, the things they liked, that you were eager, then, to give them. Even the way they kissed, made love. I remember one day in spring when I realized for the first time that grass is green. For me it was a new way of being in the world. That grass is green.

Her face as she turned toward the window was outlined in light. She turned toward me. Her eyes the color of light. I sat very still. Afraid to move. Afraid to let the moment pass. Afraid.

It is so easy to forget, to lapse into confusion. In the center, the struggle, the motion which is the center, clarity is simple. Distance, a way of constructing stories, making up lies. The easiest thing in the world — to forget, to lose the center. To fail to hold it together.

3.

How quiet the streets are at five in the morning. An old woman with a wide kerchief/plaid coat searching through the garbage cans. A young man with the Sunday *Times* curved under his arm. An Irish Setter sniffing aimlessly on the fire-escape across the street. For once, the city, quiet. Only the sound of the TV in the other room, and this typewriter:

221

You spoke in your letter of immortality. Of the loss of immortality. How well I know that fear. How it has consumed the last three years of my life. How it haunts me even now, settles in my mind, like an old diary you keep returning to, expecting it to tell you something new, reveal some mystery. The despair knowing somewhere there is an end, somewhere in the distance, undefined, there is an end, of whatever sort, after years of never dealing in beginnings and endings, of never thinking of the past and the future except as abstractions, the present being all and still all, now, even in these moments, all.

The morning is still. And dark. In the half-hour before sunrise I sit here at this desk. Grey. And then streaks of light. Waiting for the sun to rise so I can go to sleep. As I do some mornings. Somehow knowing things are different in daytime. That in daylight things move and breathe.

It was exactly three years ago today that I began to face the fact that I was mortal, vulnerable, could be hurt irrevocably, could fail.

4.

It is strange that a city can be so noisy, even a city like New York. They are tearing up Second Avenue now to put in a subway where it is not needed, when three blocks away it is needed. The noise returns promptly each morning at seven o'clock. It reminds me constantly and with great precision of that real futility, not what we each face, which is not futile, because it is real, is part of us as human beings, and as part of our own life has meaning, but that other futility, that noise, which means nothing, because it is not needed here, is not a need here, is happening here, where it is not needed, when so close to us, the need exists.

One attempts to deal with failure, but how does one learn to live with success. One tries to adjust to rejection, but how does one deal with support. With the responsibility it brings. With the necessity to act, to speak, to reveal.

Your letter, this morning, when I so desperately needed it, unexpected, reminded me again of those other people, who, like you, I swore I would never forget. Who gave reason, meaning, to my life. Because it has always been people who have given me that meaning. Not ideas, but people. As they pinpointed segments of my life. And were buried, were covered, finally, are covered, finally, with the soot, dirt, confusion of this city, the piles of newsprint, the voices, blurred, blurring, shouting out of radios, cars, TVs, mouths, noise, noise, noise...

5.

Maybe getting older simply means not taking things for granted so much anymore. In a plane this summer, after many such trips, for the first time, afraid. Seeing the world swerve beneath me. The round shell of the plane, small, somehow, not another world, but a piece located somewhere in space, in time. A gnawing in my stomach. The first symptom of fear. And below, the land, tidy, safe. Not afraid of crashing, but a more basic fear — of leaving the ground, my ground. What holds me down, secures me. Not like this. Lost against the clear morning sky. Growing older every minute. Exposed.

I think all my life I have loved women. Have been in love with what I am, what I wanted to be. With what I thought was beautiful. Gentle. With what I wanted, gently, beautifully, to touch, to be.

You can only see them in the dew. Otherwise, they're invisible. The cobwebs. Holding blades of grass together. Hundreds of them. In the early morning fog. Stretching beyond eyesight, beyond the length of eye. It was like that with us, when we were alone together. It was easy to understand why they could no longer see us, why they were no longer a part of us. Their language, their customs, all their places. Your touch — the opening, that which opened out of, which freed.

6.

For one week I have been sitting here. Trying to construct/ reconstruct a life. Trying to form, to create a life. In flashes. Fragments of heat and years. In moments of insight, confusion. For one week now I have been sitting here, in this apartment, in silence, alone. And now I can begin to move, to speak. The way a person really moves. Not step by step through a series of events, incidents, people — but layer by layer, building, forming, assimilating a life.